MW00447805

Published in the United States of America

First Printing, 2019

ISBN 978-1-6990-3699-0

Amazon.com, INC. Publishing
PO Box 81226
Seattle, Washington 98108

KDP.amazon.com

Living with Phanto*MS*

~ A Journey to The Truth ~

Living with Phanto*MS*

"A Journey to The Truth"

Author: Dawnmarie Deshaies

Editor-in-Chief:

Robert J. Deshaies II

Design & Format Directors:

Dawnmarie & Robert J. Deshaies II

Directors of Photography:

Robert Deshaies & Nancy Villere

Makeup Artist:

"Hey Saylor Cosmetic" by Noelle Sweeney

Table of Contents

Introduction:

Dear Readers,

Your life is your story. Write well and edit often.

Living with Multiple Sclerosis is an everyday challenge. I know the previous statement is quite generic, but to all those who have been diagnosed or are acquainted with the disease, we know firsthand the toll it takes upon the self, your family, and your friends.

After learning about my diagnosis in 2012, after months of contemplating the unknown path my life was about to take me on, I began to do my research compared to just what the health professionals told me. Learning that this specific auto-immune disorder is a progressive disease, I knew it would be with me for the rest of my life. Recognizing the drastic toll this disease has clamped over me only pushes me to persist and manage to continue to live a healthy and positive lifestyle.

As one can see, living with this disease; however, it's not always that simple to keep a positive attitude with the constant physical pain alongside the mental struggles brought on by the unstoppable decay. Every day is different for me. To give up on yourself and your dreams only submits yourself to the tumultuous rollercoaster of unbridled pain and misery. When depression bombards me and the thought of giving up in that all too familiar moment, I could throw in the towel, but then I realize it's up to me to control what I want to do with my life; the disease will not define me.

With the initial prognosis, I struggled for those first few months, stricken with unimaginable fear of falling and being attacked by myself, it forced me to be bedridden and afraid. After many months of familial support & self-actualization I knew these phantoms would never leave, so why not discipline myself to realize these actions and feelings and turn them for the better?

Multiple Sclerosis has made me even more determined to live my life. Not only have I accepted this disease as a part of who I am, but I also affirm it will never stop me from telling my story or living the happy and fortuitous life of love I deserve.

You deserve this life as well, and I hope my story helps you realize this for yourself.

Dedications:

To my cousin, Nick Sucy. While taken by this disease, he never let his illness take him. He lived each day to the fullest even when in his wheelchair. Here is a poem Nick wrote that I would like to share with the world:

"Flying"

It'd be awesome to be able to fly. Not in a plane, but like Superman flying. Right? Imagine the places you'd go and the great sights you could see. But you can't fly. And I can't fly.

I bet you don't hang about wishing you could fly.

I don't.

I also don't sit around wishing I could go for epic bike rides, or walk down the street to hang out, or climb mountains. If I could I would.

I can't.

It all becomes relative.

I've learned that I can't compare my life to that of others who do all those things I'd do. It'd be an exercise in futility. Even more so, it'd be an exercise in frustration.

So, who do I stack my life up against? Where do I make the comparisons?

I don't. I live.

There are more people than not who can do, but don't. They sit. They watch TV, and drink beers. Maybe, they dream of doing. Maybe, they don't. There are plenty of things I can't do, but still I do.

While they sit, I push. While they drink, I ski. While they watch, I play.

I'd be lying if I claimed I wasn't briefly bummed I couldn't have climbed that mountain. But I climb mountains every day.

While you were climbing yesterday, I pushed to campus. That's my mountain, and every time I push it, it becomes more of a hill.

On my way back from campus I was resting on the Farm Road when I was approached by a man, I happen upon occasionally on the bike path. He pointed to the steep, windy hill I just descended, and he asked me,

"How do you do those hills?"

I briefly thought about the question. I had no concerns about being cliché when I told him...

"I just do it."

~ Nick Sucy

___

To everyone who has stood by my side in my hardships, disappointments, and thank you for the continued support.

To all my fellow Multiple Sclerosis warriors, all of you who live with this disease are true heroes and warriors. Continue to inspire those around you who are also afflicted but continue to also spread thoughts of love and persistence with all afflicted by fellow auto-immune disorders.

I dedicate my thoughts and prayers, so that continued awareness can be spread, and I hope that one day we find a cure for Multiple Sclerosis. This is all for you!

Chapter 1 - Early Life & Misfortunes

My Name is Dawnmarie Deshaies, I was born &
christened in a tiny town called Old Town Maine. My
parents are John and Barbara Desjardins. I have one
sibling his name is Mark, he 4 years older than I. At the
age of 2 years old, my parents moved our family to a
small town called Baltic, Connecticut; the population was
only 800 people. My family and I lived a simple life. Both
of my parents John and Barbara, worked blue-collar jobs.
Our lifestyle produced a simple outlook on how life
should be. I was your average girl in a small town. I loved
to draw and dream of what my life would be when I got
older.

I went to school, played outside like any other kid. I loved
music, especially Queen. I was naturally silly with my
friends; we would ride our bikes and play outside for
hours on end. I had one close friend by the name of Meg.
As a young girl, I struggled with sickness and the constant
rotating door of hospital visits due to my severe Asthma.
It seemed that everything inside the house and outside

would attack me personally, often causing flare-ups with my Asthma, suctioning air from my lungs. The constant threat and fear of losing that last breath. My parents did everything they could; from taking all my stuffed toys out of my room, to putting an air conditioner in my bedroom window. The air conditioner seemed to help me breathe, especially during the winter and cold months. When my lungs began to feel crushing from constant attacks, my Parents would admit me to the hospital. The doctors would put me into what they called the green tent. It was a plastic and see-through tent pumping pure oxygen to aid my breathing. They would also administer an IV into my arm and give me medications to make my lungs healthy again. I would usually be in the hospital for over a week at a time, in the cold and sterilized place.

I began to shape my world around the idea that everything was normal. I did what my doctors told me and followed my parent's instructions to the letter. The next thing I had to go through was the dreaded allergy shots. Every week I had to revisit the doctors for a continuing series of allergy diagnoses formulating and even more disfigured version of a "normal" life.

Due to the constant hospitalizations, I missed so much school that I had to stay back in 2nd grade. How awful it was for me to discover the cruelty of my fellow classmates. The constant bullying and humiliation for being held back to due illness. The innate hatred and cruelty bestowed in every human being surrounding me burned a hole in me so deep I was retreating into myself more and more. It became tough even to crack the shell of exposing myself to the world. I began to find solace in my imagination, and I began to express all my misfortunes onto a canvas.

Chapter 2 - The Challenges of Being Different

I had a tough time learning and remembering things. Possibly because of the constant rotating medications being introduced into my system. Schoolwork was always a challenge for me, and I didn't have the confidence like all the other children around me. I struggled with feeling alienated. I always had to ask for specialized help from my teachers on my classwork. This continued throughout my young formative years of schooling. As I was becoming a young teenager, I started to have a little more confidence in myself as I grew older. These coming years were formulating to become some of the most tumultuous years of my life.

I found others like me, and we created our small circle of friendship. Unfortunately, cruelty and humiliation united us because we were all made fun of for asking for extra help with our studies. What propelled the shame even further was my fear of speaking in front of the class. When I was asked to present, I would get so nervous, and I would begin to shake, my voice shook and trembled as I spoke backward. The only thing I could hear was the endless laughter as I stood there defenseless.

Every day as lunchtime rolled around, my friends and I would all go out to the playground, and the kids would make it a mission to come up to me and belittle me by calling me, "stupid, dumb, and brainless." I looked away in shame and cried a river wondering how the world can be so cruel to a little girl trying just to live? Cruelty, as I have come to learn, is unfortunately inherent in the human psyche. Often, it is easier to give in and feed the beast, but turning away and showing your belittler compassion instead of hate will make the other hunger for the common ground.

With the constant humiliation and belittling, I forced myself to study harder and longer to prove that I am better if not equal to all the people chastening me. I had my favorite teachers who worked with me and helped me grow in my studies, they knew how hard it was on me to be in and out of the hospital all the time. Their sympathy and willingness to aid me helped me imagine that the world can be a better place to continue living in. The first spark of hope in a mad world.

One teacher, Mrs. Johnson, used to make me laugh no matter what emotional state I was in. I remember her saying to me one day, "Oh, don't listen to them Dawnmarie, one day you will be amazing, and then they will wonder why they were so mean to you." She always helped me learn in a way that made sense to me. I really liked Mrs. Johnson's work, and I could not help but admire her work with all the other kids struggling just like me. Thinking about my younger self now, I have made it a personal affirmation to use laughter and love to teach those around me.

Chapter 3 - Treasured Memories

I remember every summer we would go to Maine to see my Grandparents and all my cousins. I loved this particular time of year. I had so many cousins I often lost count. I had my favorite cousins surrounding me and encouraging me to come to play. They were my best friends from afar. Their father was my mother's brother. His name was Uncle Shorty and his wife, Aunt Gretchen. They had three girls, Lisa, Tabitha, and Stacy. Every time we would visit them, it was the best time of my life. All the activities we would do included playing hide and seek, singing "You've Got a Friend in Me" by Randy Newman, painting our own Monet's, climbing bountiful trees filled with fresh pinecones. We would go down to the corner store get soda and candy, and on a scorching day, we would get ice cream. You name it, we did it. These were indeed some of my favorite times in my life as a young child. The endless groove from the music, the love for one another, and the incapacitating sugar rushes will never be forgotten. It was always hard to leave after our vacation had ended. I pondered, why can't the world be like this never-ending fairytale.

I can remember we always had big family gatherings. My mother had three sisters and six brothers. My father had four brothers and five sisters. Honestly, I still have no idea how many cousins I had. All I remember is I loved every minute I spent with all of them. My summers were as perfect as a freshly bloomed sunflower, I was glowing with love and happiness. The pain of the school year being washed away with each giggle and laugh.

My Grammy, my mother's mom, was the cutest grandmother anyone could ever imagine. I would miss her so much every time we drove from her porch as I waved my hands out the car window. Every time we were able to visit her in Maine, she would let me bake with her. The sweet smell of freshly made whoopee pies and cinnamon rolls from an old family recipe filled the room with this iridescent energy. My Grammy was so funny she had no teeth, and every time we would visit, she would always say, "I am going to gum you to death munchkin, nom, nom, nom." I would giggle and hustle to the nearest escape, but she always caught me. She always made me feel so loved. I really miss her. While staying at her house, I always got to stay in the back bedroom. It was my perfect little haven. My mother's father had passed away before I was born, so Grammy was my connection to my history. My mother is the youngest of her family, all though she had a baby brother he was the only one born in a hospital and he only lived for two days.

All my Aunts and Uncles had such a great sense of humor. I believe that to this day it has impacted me always to be silly and fun-loving, because who doesn't love a joyful spirit? When looking back on these memories, I see the big picture of how I began to formulate my self-image. Positive attracts positive, so spread your joy because you will meet others who can share it with you.

My father's mother was always fun, but more along the lines of Grace Kelly in the iconic 1955 film "To Catch a

Thief" by Alfred Hitchcock. She really didn't play with us very much she was much more proper and would be socializing with all the adults. I never met my father's father he also passed away before I was born. I still thank God to this day for what he gave me growing up. I was blessed with two amazing grandmothers, numerous Aunts and Uncles, and the continually multiplying cousins. Oh, me oh, my.

Every time we visited Maine, my aunts and uncles would ask so many questions about my brother and me. I believed they liked me better (wink's face). My favorite aunt Theresa and her husband, uncle Bob, were so hilarious. My uncle Bob would always say, "Hey, baby girl come over here so I can see how much you have grown." I would giggle and smile. Then he would always say pull my finger. So, I did, and he would make the funniest fake farting noise; I could not help but burst into laughter, sometimes I even tinkled my pants. My aunt Theresa was always cooking and baking and still had so many pets, like birds, cats, and dogs. Her house had so many Knick knacks like ceramic angels, animals, and clocks. Her refrigerator was full of photos and artwork. I loved my Aunt Theresa so much she was always so funny and very affectionate to everyone. She would yell at my uncle Bob all the time, especially when he tried to sing over our favorite musician, Elvis Presley. That was so funny to me. He would always say, "woman, you need to find your place!" and she would say, "come and make me." I believe this is where my sass and spunk originated from. Oh, how I was and still am a troublemaker.

My Aunt Theresa would always let me do her hair and paint her figure nails. I simply loved the feeling of being wanted and loved. This made me feel important. She would always give me my own room to sleep in because of my asthma she had an air conditioner in there, and it would help me breath better. I never knew why it helped me breath better, but she was always caring for me in those little ways. Aunt Theresa would always be painting; she had a small art gallery upstairs. I loved that and thought it was the coolest room in the house. I loved painting and drawing; she would always say that I was a great artist. She always encouraged me to paint and draw every time I would visit. Sometimes, I wish those humble summers would last forever because I was able to laugh play and be me when we visited Maine.

On my dad's side of the family, I had favorites too. My aunt Franny and aunt Anne, aunt Sue, and aunt Tessie they were all so cool. My aunt Sue and uncle Mac lived in Connecticut as well. We visited my aunt Sue often. She was always so sweet and kind. I loved all my aunts and uncles. Having a large family was nice because we always had someone to visit and catch up with. My aunt Dell lived in Connecticut. She married my mother's brother. My uncle Dicky would always stop by our house on his way home from work to pee and get coffee from our house. He was a junkyard junkie and a massive hoarder. His van always had so many treasures in it, from chairs, tables, and just plain old junk. Every time we would visit them, which was often, my aunt Dell would be making the most beautiful wedding and birthday cakes. I remember loving to visit her so much because of all the excellent food and delicious smells of fresh baked goods. We always had Thanksgiving dinner at their home because let's face it who doesn't love a home-cooked meal from scratch? She was the best cook ever; I will place money on it every time. My aunt and uncle had a big house they had two sons and two daughters. I would always stay in the house and visit with my mom. When I wasn't having an asthma attack, my mother would let me go outside to climb in the trees with my cousins and their friends, ah how I miss the smell of those fresh pines. We would play hide and seek; the best part was their basement because it had so much junk in it that you could disappear for hours, sometimes I would even get scared because of all the little creeks and hollow noises. I loved playing with them, we would sing and laugh for hours. We would ride bikes around the small town where they lived, and they also had a pool, so when summer rolled around, we would always visit and swim. Alas, even with the endless joys of summer, my illness was still lingering in the background. The doctors simply told my mother and me it was just my allergies. I hated those words because they seemed like an excuse at the time for something wrong with me.

Chapter 4 – Not Everything Can be Perfect

Both of my parents smoked cigarettes, so that didn't help my breathing back then. Smoking was a part of the culture; it was thought to be filled with nutritious vitamins and minerals. How things have changed. I still to this day have never touched a cigarette in my life. I was always feeling different from all the kids around me from my friends to my cousins. I was the sick child, the little wilted flower no one wanted to pick. in and out, in and out. The emotionless hospital & the isolated green tent were the second home I was used to. I wanted to be able to do a breath. It was a time of constant rotating medications. When the hospital would send me home after a week, my lungs felt better, but my mom would always be worried about me. I worried about her.

Every time I would have an Asthma attack, I would have to go into my bedroom to breath better. Somedays, my mom, would take me out shopping at the mall because they had air conditioning and that meant we didn't have to pay for it…. And sometimes she would let me pick out clothing, and we would put it on layaway. My mom would go into the store and make payments until it was all paid for, and when that happened, it was like Christmas to me. I would have new clothes and shoes. This was before they had credit cards, they had layaway. To me, this seemed normal. Both of my parents worked so hard. To make ends meet. I remember when my Dad had lower back surgery, and he was out of work for the longest time. We had our family car repossessed, and that made things so hard on my mom she was working double-time to keep a roof over our heads.

I can remember eating fried bologna and Bologna sandwiches with chips. And my mom always had Pepsi soda in the house and T.V. microwaved dinners to be honest; my mother wasn't an excellent cook, and she didn't have the time to cook. My mother worked so hard all the time and was so tired from working hard that when she got home, she was utterly exhausted. We just made sandwiches and had microwave dinners.

My Best friend Meg always had the newest and most beautiful clothing, and her mom stayed home and took care of the house. Sometimes her mom would make me a dress. I really liked hanging out with Meg; we also went to the same school. We both made the cheerleading team together; we loved it and felt like we were fitting in with the other girls. I began to perceive that some aspects of self-confidence began to flower.

Chapter 5 - My First Job

I had my first job at Penny's, a store in Norwich. It was convenient being so close to home. I would work after school. I was 15 years old. I grew up knowing you had to work hard for your money and to never take things for granted. Seeing how all my other friend's moms stayed home to take care of the kids would make me blue that my mother had to work so hard. She worked in a warehouse job doing screen printing by hand with other working women. I would ride my bike down to her work after school because I really loved watching all the colors spraying and splashing the yards of canvas, turning the seemingly endless rainbow barrage into the most wondrous clothing. There were so many giant rolls of fabric with thousands of different prints ready to be shipped out to clothing companies, and my mother was one of the many women who worked for hours and days creating such beautiful pieces of fabric. The designers should be lucky to have her employed, without her, the prints would be just blank canvas.

I love my mother; she always told me how to work hard for a living even when you didn't want to work. Her hands would be swollen from hard labor all day in an unconditioned hot factory. The smell of paint in the air stained her hair in the skin, bringing home a mixture of scents. These factories never had to air-condition, with all the women working so hard, it made me wonder how is it that until these last few years women are now getting the right to work in a proper workplace. When I would visit my mother at work, everyone one of her friends would always tell me I was going places. This beautiful regard baffled me back then because I never really imagined or knew what they meant? Having been raised by my mother primarily, I constructed my own thoughts on work ethic, and my mother was the cornerstone for that belief. Thank you, mom, for making me realize if I wanted something, I needed to work for it. Your persistence is a gift I still hold onto today. Even growing up with Asthma, I never made an excuse for it. It was just something I had to deal with. Put a smile on your face and work hard. I learned this very early on in my life because I didn't want to be different, so I would always smile and push through whatever was going on in my life. I just wanted to feel normal, many years later, I learned normal isn't always the best choice nor option.

Chapter 6 - High school, Young Adulthood, Emerging Phantoms & Dreams

As my adolescence continued, I attended Norwich Academy of Fine Arts. From the age of thirteen to eighteen, this school impacted me in ways that helped me make the most of my life during this time. I went to work after school every day. I liked my job because I was making money for myself, but I loved everything about school. My passions resided in learning. I treasured all my fine art classes, and I had my favorite teachers instructing these classes. I felt the alive painting. My inspiration for designing a love language in my own artistic fashion pushed my imagination to the limits. I began to imagine myself as one of the masters of Impressionist & Renaissance art like Van Gogh, Monet, and Da Vinci. While studying the work of the masters, I picked each individual detail that I admired from so many artists and developed my own art style. I created beauty with a black canvas, the art that poured from my fingertips struck me with emotion with each stroke. I poured everything into my art. The good, the bad, the ugly all represented aspects of my being expunged onto the canvas. My three favorite artists are Claude Monet, Leonardo Da Vinci, and Vincent Van Gogh. I always enjoyed reading their history and admiring their life works, could it be possible that I can create my own legacy of design? I hope to share my art with the world so you can see me for who I am, my mind is as beautiful as my body.

From admiring their works, I promised myself and my teachers that I will make it Paris one day to self-actualize my belief in becoming a master by studying the physical copies existing in the art capital of the world. They would always smile and say, "I hope so Dawnmarie, your work needs to be seen and admired." To this very day, I still have some of my old drawings and painting from school, and my mother still has some of her favorites as well.

Art classes made me feel so alive and vibrant. I had a special bond with all the art students. The constant influx of sharing ideas and discussing different techniques boosted my creativity always to continue developing new pieces of work. My classmates and I still hung out together. We had lunch together and always did things on the weekends for school projects for art classes. I began to achieve A's in all my classes. From working hard in my studies and out of school to keep a B+, I managed to stay above to average grades with a 3.0 all 4 years and worked 25 hours a week as well.

Of course, some of you are probably wondering about my early love life. Well, I dated the same boy for over 5 years; his name was John. I honestly thought he was the person I was going to marry; he even gave me an engagement ring after graduating from Art school. He was all I knew between school, working, and everyday life.

After graduating from school, I moved out of my parents' home and got my own apartment there weren't any jobs in the art field and I had to pay bills, so I started working in New London, Connecticut. I worked at the mall fulltime, and before I knew it, I was an Assistant

Manager. My career was moving fast, I was promoted again to a larger store as the Manager, after just 6 months. I was engaged to John, but I knew deep down inside I wanted more in my life. I had dreams of still being a princess taken away by a knight in shining armor, and he wasn't taking my breath away from the way I needed it. His dreams did not resonate with me, and I didn't want to settle for anything less. It was hard breaking up with him. First love is a confusing game. It's a maze of discovery and contemplation. Which choice should I make when I have an engagement ring on my finger, but I cannot imagine a future with this person, so he obviously could not be the one? He was my only boyfriend; I lost my virginity to him, and I loved him, but love and desire are often intertwined with each other, and it's hard to separate the two especially at such a young age. He worked hard, but he never really had plans to move and make something of himself. He was comfortable, and I wanted more for my life. I realized that if he loved me, he would follow, but he didn't so I let him go. I had bigger plans for myself and my dreams.

I had so many dreams as a young Woman graduating from school, I thought after high school and college, I was going to move to New York City. Well little did I know it was so hard to get into the doors of any design company or even any art studios. You had to know someone in the field already working there, and I didn't know anyone. Working in retail, I was able to use my design background to work on floor moves and designs for the stores. I implemented myself where I could, and I enjoyed using my art background where I could, but I knew I could achieve more with my prowess.

I really enjoyed my job and the like before I was asked to move to a new company called Butler shoes. They moved me to their big store in New London, Connecticut. I worked with them for two years, and then another company recruited me. The company was called Rainbow shops; it was a women's apparel company. As an area manager, I was running five stores. I was working long hours and traveled a lot. Looking back today on my life at the time, I saw my work ethic being tested, and I never gave up. As my Asthma attacks lingered from childhood, they intruded less and less as I grew older.

As I continued working and traveling, I believe my symptoms for an early prognosis MS started to show itself. I would be organizing floor moves, in all the stores during after-hours when I began to lose feeling in my hands like pins and needles were silently pressing onto my skin. I started to drop things as I worked like my muscles just let go, and I had no idea why I just make it happen. My vision also became blurred during strenuous activity, but with all these symptoms starting to arise, I figured working long hard hours, much like anyone else, were a result of excessive tiredness. So, I kept on moving along with that smile on my face. The same smile I learned so early on to hide the pain of all my other woes.

As with all things, my life continued, despite my body sending me constant feedback to slow down the continuous wave of work. With my mother's words resonating in the back of my head, "never give up, you need to keep moving forward," I pushed through the pain which at the time was far away from what I began to feel later. With such a small amount of life under my belt, working was pretty much all I knew at the time. I thought that if I continued improving my career, I would become the success I dreamed about so much since I was a child. If I was sick, I still pulled myself from underneath the sheets because bills still need to be paid, and without working that would never happen. Like mom said, "smile like you have nothing to worry about." With the growing confidence of an up and coming career, nothing was going to slow me down.

Chapter 7 – Climbing the Career Ladder

At a ripe old age of 20 years, I was recruited again by another prevalent company at the come titled Rave, another women's apparel store. The most significant decision by accepting this new job was my move to Springfield, Massachusetts. So, here I was jumping into the unknown of exciting possibilities. I rented a room in a quaint New England house at the time until I found an apartment and a roommate to pair myself with. Everything was going so well; the move was perfect & I wasn't stressed with the crushing workload as I was beforehand. As Spring rolled around in the warm month of May, with all the change in the air, I bought a new car to signify the big move and increased confidence in my ability. It was a Honda Civic colored baby blue, I absolutely loved it.

Most importantly, though, it was "my" car. I used the money I had been working for the last couple of years to buy this for myself. How wonderful it was to drive with that new car smell. The sweet scent of change and accomplishment all in one. The job was going great. I was living in what I thought was a perfect life. With increased confidence, I was walking taller than I really was, you know like the old saying, "when a woman straps on her heels, she becomes the queen of the world." With a cup of coffee in my hand, and the biggest smile on my face as I rolled into work in this cute, baby blue Honda, I strutted down my imaginary runway to stardom. The new arrival of passion for life was only slightly hindered by the increasing workload. I knew life couldn't always be perfect and I had to make the most of it as I went along, but this was the most I could reach for at the time, and I believe I made the most of it.

The change was ever-present in Massachusetts. Seasons increased rain, and my allergies blowing the roof off my apartment was causing my asthma to act up again. So, living with my roommate and without the guidance of my mother, I went to the hospital. They gave me a new medication called Albuterol. This made things easier for me when I was having trouble. The phantoms began resurrecting within me, and the feelings of my hands and feet falling asleep along with my problems in my vision began to rear their ugly heads again. I just thought this must be my normal behavior when exposed to excess stress. Looking back on my sickly childhood, I thought this was completely normal and just soldiered on.

As the tides changed and the world kept rotating on its axis, I made new friends and really felt like I was making a great life for myself. I became the area sales manager for the second time in my career having 5 stores to manage all around Massachusetts and began to travel a lot more with work just like before. I worked the weekly forty hours along with numerous hours of overtime, and yet, I kept my smile strong and stayed positive because I really liked my job. For all those beginning in their career, I hope you find something you love doing because it makes life so much easier when you enjoy the work you are managing. You will reach your dreams.

Floor plans were changing every week on headquarters decision, new marketing campaigns were beginning to float to the surface every couple of months, and new merchandise meant we had to make the store look perfect to a wide range of customers. I also began to work on accounting sales margins per request of the higher-ups. Numbers and margins became the norm for me, I was making sure every store was meeting their weekly and monthly sales goals. My team was easy and fun. Luckily, I was working with all women, so, the gossip was continually flowing. Girls, after all, just want to have fun.

I really loved working with people. We managed to work hard and still make the workplace fun. I could sell anything to anyone; if someone asked for advice on what to wear, I could sell them a leaf patch, and they would leave thinking it was Chanel. I was that good. Working in retail was a great experience, I believe every person should work in retail once due to working most weekends and holidays. Retail work teaches you how to interact with all kinds of people and gives you confidence when you begin to sell in increased margins. Besides all the numbers and margins, I really cared for all my customers. To simply bring a smile to someone's face after helping them find the perfect outfit would make my day. I really enjoyed making others feel confident in themselves, and I hope to inspire all women to feel like a queen or a princess even on their worst days. I smiled while handing them their bag of new accessories and clothing, and always felt the warm exchange of joy piercing our two faces. By instilling confidence in another, I found it in myself.

My teams were amazing, and working with so many different personalities intrigued and fascinated me. As a manager, I would motivate them daily and made work fun to keep up the bravado. I would like to think I was a fun boss but also astute in getting the job done. I guess you could say I was a no-nonsense boss. I worked about sixty-five to seventy hours a week traveling from store to store working with my sales teams and really getting to know them and what their lives were like. They were my work family, and I loved every second spent with them.

I remember days, I would collapse into my couch because the phantom fatigue crept in as soon as I stepped from my car and into my apartment. When I wasn't at work or around anyone, I would wonder why there were so many things wrong with me. Was life really supposed to be this normal? To live with a constant wave of unknown agony. I began to talk to my co-workers about my symptoms, and they would say, "Dawnmarie, sweetie, you are working too hard, take a vacation." Following a couple more weeks of enduring pain, I went in for a checkup with a local doctor. In concurrence with my co-workers, the doc said, "take a vacation Dawnmarie." All my blood work returned normal, so the only physically present ailment was my asthma. I continued to lie to myself, encouraging myself that the pains were just the stress of working. That lie only made me worry more because I knew deep down, I wasn't supposed to be feeling this way all the time. I redirected my focus to work, pushing my own health to the side most of the time. I was a hard worker, and I was determined as ever to be the best district sales manager ever! Even if I wasn't feeling well, I was never going to let anything stop me. I never really went out too much due to workload, but one day the girls said let's go out for a drink and my whole life changed again.

Chapter 8 - Turning *Twenty-One*

I was finally 21 years old, so let the roaring '20s begins again. It was time to hit the town with my ladies. Of course, I was always looking fabulous because who doesn't need a day to feel themselves. I met so many people and tried to balance my work life and personal life. I met a police officer; his name was Thomas; we hit it off and started dating. I met his sister Nancy; she was a nurse, and we got along great. I was all about working hard and climbing the corporate ladder, so love wasn't as prevalent in my mind, it was a time to concentrate on work and find time to let loose.

Continuing to live in Massachusetts was ok. The weather seemed to bother my Asthma a lot, and the strange phantom symptoms continued to fatigue and tire me out day today. Life carried on. I continued to work, date, and go out with friends. I dated Thomas for over a year, and I started to live with his sister Nancy. We became great friends and always strolled to night clubs and bars together with our friends after work. I knew this wasn't all I wanted to do with my life, I still had bigger dreams for my life I wanted to travel the world, paint murals and own my own business working on interior design one day.

My bucket list at the time consisted of jumping out of a plane, learning to fire a weapon (like Lara Croft), wanting to teach children to paint and draw, traveling to the artistic capitals of the world to see all my idol's work, relax on a secluded beach drinking a bottle of Champagne, and paint my own work for the world to see. Most of all, I wanted to start my own business, I wanted to model people's homes, and I wanted to model in them as well. From being a mere five feet two inches (like one of my favorite artists currently: Lady Gaga), the last check was a long-stretched dream, but I never gave up on it. Of course, I was still on the hunt for my Prince charming. I knew one day I would settle down and start a family so I could pass along all my artistic visions and create a life of love and adoration for my own children. I hoped to pass along all the incredible life lessons I had learned so far, such as my inherent compassion for all living things and my impeccable work ethic. I wanted to raise influential Individuals, who could take care of themselves and spread a kind message for the world to see with their talents. I wanted to be a leader and make a difference in people's lives. I'm still working on being a leader to this day.

When I gave my mother, father, and teachers this list, they all said to me, you can do whatever your heart desires in life. It takes determination and hard work. I had accomplished so much at such a young age already, and I was not going to stop there. My relationship with Thomas only lasted one year, it wasn't a natural break-up. He was seeing other people, and I was only seeing him, the signs of an immature man, not knowing what he wants in life. I thought to my self was I really in love with him? Or was it just comfortable having someone in my life? Looking back now, I'm glad I was able to answer such substantial life questions at the time. He moved on with his life, and I moved on with mine. I moved out from Nancy's home, and I even attended her wedding party as a maid of honor. She married her best friend, Bill. Bill and

Nancy made a great couple, and they knew how to live life and have fun.

Chapter 9 - The New Move

After Bill & Nancy's wedding, I moved out and found a new apartment to live in just around the corner. I stopped going out at night and continued growth in my career. At the end of long days, I would go home shower and go to sleep, I always was so fatigued. I worked so much that my girlfriends finally said, "you're coming out for a drink with us Dawnmarie, you need a little dancing to boost you up." I needed to get back to my roots. I needed to remind myself how to be silly and have fun. Life isn't all about work! I decided to go out with them this one night, we went to a new hotel in town, The Sheraton Hotel. They had a small night club, so off we went, with our hoops in our ears, our hair flawless, and that look in eyes that resembled the passion of Aphrodite.

When we arrived, we strolled to the bar and ordered some drinks. With music blaring in our ears, all my friends were picked off one by one. Each man coming up more handsome than the last asking for a hand to dance with, but not me. I thought ok Dawnmarie you have hit rock bottom; how could I be looking so regal and elegant and no man has swooped me off my feet. Maybe it was the liquor in me, but I was feeling myself.

Little did know on the other side of the club, there was a very hot, sexy, young man. Little to my knowledge at the time was holding off all his friends from approaching me. So, my fun levels were drowning, and I told my girlfriends I was going to go home. Talk about feeling unattractive and unwanted at the age of 21, "wow!" I thought to myself. I said, "at least I still have a job that loves me"! I loved working and being confident. My job made me come alive daily being able to work with new and potently extravagant people. I learned to look at life as a fresh start every day, no matter how I was feeling.

Chapter 10 – Mr. Tall, Dark, & Handsome

As I was leaving with a glum outlook on the nite, this tall, dark and handsome man with a smile that could melt your heart came up to me and asked me to dance. It was the moment I was looking forward to the whole night, so of course, I said "yes," with an unbridled glee in my voice. I was trying to keep my cool, but he knew he had me roped in. He whispered in my ear, "I have been watching you all night, and my friends have helped me stop everyone who came next to you." At first, I laughed, then I realized he was kidding. We laughed and danced. As he pulled close and closer, he asked me where I worked. I told him I was a traveling woman; I worked as a district sales manager. He proceeded to ask where exactly I spent most of the time in that gentle, all too charming voice. Without restraint, I told him I would be at the Holyoke Mall in Massachusetts. For the next week, he asked for my phone number, I said no. I never give my number out to strangers. He looked at me and pondered why? I sweetly said, "goodbye," looked him in the eyes and smiled. Then I walked out and went home with a smile on my face. I knew how to play this game, but lingering in the back of my head, I knew I had already lost myself to him.

The very next day I was in one of my stores working on the payroll books, and all a sudden he comes walking in the store, Mr. sharp-dressed man. His name was Robert, the man from the night club last night with two dozen red roses in his hand. I was shocked and didn't expect it. I smiled and blushed at the same time and thought to myself wow I guess I still have it. We talked a little he asked if he could take me out on a date I said yes. It was June 11th, 1988, our first date. That lingering thought from the night before knew it was all over. Could he be the one?

He called and said, "I am picking you up, and we are going out on my boat," I said, "ok.", he asked if I knew how to water ski I said, "no." I was so nervous, but my desire for adventure was bursting through my brain. I have always been ready for adventures in my life, and I never say no to a new challenge. So, I told myself, "Eh,

what the hell I need to live life, or it will pass me by."
Robert picked me, punctual as always, and up and off we
went to the lake. His boat was waiting for us, floating in
the calm lake as the sun gleamed down on us. He had
asked his good friend and his girlfriend to meet us there,
Dani and Rose, childhood friends of Robert. They seemed
nice. We had lunch, and we all went out on the skis
afterward. At first, I was scared I wouldn't be able to pull
myself out of the water, but surprisingly, I was skiing
before I knew it. The rush exhilarated me, I thought,
"Holy shit, I'm skiing across the water right now," and
then suddenly, another boat comes past us and the
waves came crashing over me. I went down and snapped
my neck backward as fell and skipped into the water. In a
quick moment of fear, I felt warm arms wrap around me,
lifting me from the sea. Robert had jumped into the
water swam up with power and grace, he pulled me out
of the water effortlessly. With my nerves racked and my
body in a slight haze, I spoke to Robert asking him to take
us back to shore. Robert was so sweet he put a towel
around me and calmed me down, he said, "as long as I

get to take care of you the rest of the nite." The charm of this man!

That night we went out to dinner and a movie. I was feeling sore, and my neck really hurt, but the date was going well I didn't want to tell him I was hurting from the crash in the water, so I put a smile on my face and went. The movie was hysterical; I think all the laughing helped with the pain. It was called "The Great Outdoors" by Howard Deutch, starring John Candy and Dan Aykroyd. After the movie was over, I asked to go home. I was holding my neck from the pain and Robert asked me if I was ok. When I told him how painful it was, he said we need to go to the hospital to have you checked out. So off we went. How did an average day become a day of excitement and terror? It took them 6 hours in the ER just to be seen by a doctor they checked me out and did x-rays, and they told me I had whiplash and they put me in a neck collar and pain medication to help me get through the days at work. Talk about a thrilling first date. Robert drove me home the next morning. I was in so much pain that I couldn't go to work. Robert came over to check up on me and bring me food. He was so sweet and kind.

For the next 2 weeks, we were together every day having romantic dinners getting to know each other. We had a real connection that I never felt before he walked into my life with such power and grace. I had only been with two other men in my life before, one was my longtime boyfriend from high school I dated him for 5 years his name was John, and the other one was Thomas for one year. Neither of them made me feel like this. I had sweaty palms, and butterfly's in my stomach; is this what pregnancy felt like? Being with Robert was so easy I remember the first time we made love it felt like we were made for each other it was so passionate. And so intense he kissed me like no one before. He caressed my body like he was sculpting a masterpiece. I had shivers all over my body. I had never felt like this before, we made love for hours. We continued to make love as we showered together and he washed my hair, and then he turned me around he held my face and said, "you are so beautiful and angelic, I love everything about you. I love looking at you and feeling your body against mine". He whispered in my ear, "We were made for each, and I finally found you." We hugged for the longest time. Standing in the shower as the water ran down our bodies. That night Robert slept over.

Almost every night after that, we couldn't get enough of each other. If I were working, he would come to visit me. When I wasn't working, we were off doing something exploring the small towns around Massachusetts and making incredible memories. We would laugh all the time and hold hands as we would walk around. Anyone could spot our passion for each other from a mile away.

Chapter 11 - The Letter

I'll always remember a special moment between Robert and me when I arrived home from a regular old afternoon after work. As I walked from my car to the doorstep, I looked for my keys in my purse. Unaware of my surroundings, I suddenly bumped into Robert standing on my porch. At first, I was startled, but my anxiety soon fell away as I looked at his incredible smile. He then spoke, "Dawnmarie, I have something to give you...", and as he spoke, he held my hand and gifted me a hand-written letter. Of course - it was addressed to me, from Robert. I kept the letter in my hand and peeled open the manila envelope. In the most eloquent writing, it stated:

A woman who comes from dreams of fallen hope Dreams of a man whom had given up his pursuit of his fairy tale.

As I gaze upon her, there is so much to see.

Her every move no matter how small displays her gleam and beauty thought out the space she holds

 She leaves me breathless.

Her beauty is unrivaled by the most beautiful of all women in this man's intuitive eyes, the caves of her body and face are such that only a Maestros could have created in his greatest imagination.

While her eyes wild sparkle which cannot even be held by the brightest star on the darkest of nights

Her thoughtfulness and care for the people she loves leads me only to hope that I someday will also have love as mine.

Every day since we have met has gone like this.

I awake in the morning with thoughts of her still fresh from the night. Rushing her image to my consciousness.

The image of my princess is beckoned by the heart. I am called by a force to reach her so that I may hear her voice.

The sounds of voice fills me contentment and a desire fills me grows stronger then the previous day.

As the days goes on, the thoughts of her linger in my mind like the scent of a wild rose with a touch of morning dew. My longing for her grows.

I grow to the point of frustration

But I begin to count the days and minutes knowing that soon I will touch my radiant dream. When finally, we touch the long waiting is silenced and overwhelmed by the beating of my heart.

The touch has sent a feeling which escapes all words

Can she be the ONE?.......

R.J. Deshaies signed July 21st, 1988

Chapter 12 - First Two Weeks

After a mere two weeks of dating, Robert asked me to marry him. At first, it was an incredible shock, and my mind raced with crazy emotions. I couldn't pinpoint the exact feeling during that moment, so let's just say all of them. At this time, I withheld from deciding and made him wait for an answer. Robert was always a gentleman I felt like we couldn't get enough of each other. Our love was so passionate and real. I would be at work, and all I could do was think of him.

Every minute we had together, we became inseparable. Then Robert asked me to meet his Mother Judith, she was also an artist, and Robert took us out to lunch to get to know each other. Everything went well. Then, I met his younger brother Donald and his Grandparents from his mother's side of the family. His grandfather's name was Roland, and his grandmothers were Simone. Hold onto that name for a future reference. On this side of Robert's family, he had four aunts. Their names were Peggie, Vivian, Diane, and an uncle, Roland. On Robert's father's side of the family, he had one aunt Larine and one uncle Roger and his grandmother Jean. His grandfather Donald passed away before I came into the picture.

Robert had many friends in Springfield, Massachusetts, and was well-known throughout the small town. We both worked, and when we had days off, we were always together. Robert's best friend since childhood was a man by the name of Anthony Bradley. Anthony's family was a second family to Robert, his brother, and his mother. Robert's parents divorced long before I met Robert. He was a young boy entitled to running his family at such a young age. He was the most mature of his friends. I think it was because of the pressures piled onto him as a child. Robert also had many jobs and knew what it was like to work for something you wanted in life. We both had the same work ethic, another characteristic we both admired in each other. We continued to meet each other friends. They all said we were moving too fast, but we knew better and didn't really care how they felt. When you know, you know. Don't ever let someone try and tell you to overlook a decision. Especially when everything from your soul to your body tells you, "yes." Robert also met my family: John, Barbara, and my brother Mark. He also met some of my beloved aunts and uncles.

Everything was going so well, and work was great for me. Robert ran and operated his own jewelry company. Robert lived at home with His Mother when we met. Before that, he lived in Maryland but had been in a terrible car crash and moved home after his surgery to recover. Robert's mother worked hard to make ends meet for her family. She was a single mother raising two young boys all by herself. Judith raised both of her sons to be independent and always to take care of their family. A trait I still hold dear to my heart that I have instilled upon my children. Donald, Robert's younger brother, went off to college in Washington. So, it was just Robert and his mother in the house. Robert took care of his mom whenever she needed help. He was raised to be a gentleman and to take care of his family under any circumstances. Even at such a young age of seven years old. Robert was also brought up with similar morals and work ethic I had grown up with as well. He was a kind person and recognized early on that what you put out into the universe with positive intention will return with rewards second fold.

There were so many things I loved about Robert; he was a genuine born leader with the heart of a lion. He was passionate, generous, and warm-hearted. He led his pride with honor & elegance. He was constantly cheerful and humorous. Like any king of the pride, he was very stubborn just like me, his future queen.

Chapter 13 - Christmas Day

We dated for a year, and he proposed to me again on Christmas Day. I remember it as if it was yesterday. It was Christmas morning at his mother's house. As Robert was giving me my presents, he handed me this giant teddy bear. With glee in my voice, I was so happy to have this cute and fluffy bear to cuddle with. Little to my awareness, everyone in the room was staring at me. I looked at Donald, then Judith, Robert, and he glanced down at the velvet bow on the teddy bear, and I saw the most beautiful diamond ring. With an enormous amount of joy and pure delight in my voice, I said, "yes, I will marry you." Life was good.

I would see my friends every now and then. I was the only one engaged to be married at the time all my girlfriends were still single. My work was going well. My love life was going great, and I felt like I was living in a dream. I moved into Robert's mother's house to save money. This made it easy to plan the wedding together, even with us both working 60 plus hours a week. I started to notice I was feeling off again. The phantom pains were coming back, and I was having trouble with hold onto things like a cup of coffee. My hand would go numb all the time to the point of not being able to hold anything. It was crippling, but Robert was always there holding me if my phantoms attacked too much. I was getting a lot of headaches behind my eyes, I continued to believe they were migraines and the clusters of black spots in my vision distracted me a lot, forcing me to rest. I decided to go visit the eye doctor, and they said I had 20 20 vision. I told Robert about it, and we both thought maybe it was just stress. Remember, I was working overtime, planning our dream wedding, and running on little sleep. Thank the lord for caffeine.

So, once again, no real answers were brought to the fold. The crazy phantoms of pain and fatigue going on in my body continued to run amuck. Robert and I were planning the wedding when my stress continued to increase. My phantoms were always lurking in the back of my mind. They were getting worse. My moods were all over the place. I remember we were fighting over silly things I was so emotional all the time, a warning of what it was going to be like during pregnancy. Robert was worried about me and continued telling me not to stress; this would make me so mad because he didn't understand what was happing to me. Unfortunately, with all the misplaced anger, I couldn't explain it either. I don't know why, well yes, I do after years of self-perception and analysis, I didn't like people telling me what to do. I was so stubborn, and I always wanted to able to do it all. We are all human; we carry flaws with us since childhood. Learn to recognize your shortcomings and instead of feeding them, understand them, and correct them. Self-analysis was and has continued to always be helpful in my life. The feelings of others trying to hold me back from or controlling my decisions will always be one of my biggest transgressors. I was like a black stallion wild and free, but a hard worker and loyal.

Robert also didn't like it when I wanted to go out with my girlfriends for a drink. His flaw, much like my own, was his need for attention and consistent love. Jealousy, an all-too-human trait, meant Robert wanted me to be his and no one else's. He has improved dramatically over the years because jealousy is a young man's game. Loss of control in my life was forcing me to feel confined; everyone was telling me what to do when to do it, and how to do it. I never really understood this about me at all, but I have continued to figure out my inherent flaws. All I knew was when I felt pushed into a corner, I would push back even harder. I moved out of his house and moved into an apartment with my friend Elaine. I felt this would be better for us, without me living in his mother's house. I needed my own space to think and to feel like Robert and everybody involved in the wedding weren't trying to control me. He was always good at fixing broken things, but you can't fix everything. I knew I needed to have my own space to think things through and plan our future.

Chapter 14 – The Breakup

A couple months before the wedding, I placed the plans on hold. I felt like things were moving too fast, and being honest, I feared losing myself. Who would I be after I got married this was the question? Would I still be loyal to my inherent nature? I sure as hell wasn't going to change anything about myself to be the perfect wife. If Robert really loved me, he would accept me for how I was. He would never try to band-aid my body and mind up, no matter how hard his instinct was urging to fix an elegant piece of art like myself. I kept asking myself would I be just a housewife and do whatever Robert told me. I didn't want to lose my independence. I thought if I was meant to be single forever because I couldn't find a happy medium, then I thought I could be content with my life. Even with these emerging thoughts and questions, I really loved Robert. I didn't like feeling like he was controlling me. I thought long and hard, and this was not easy for me. At the time, I thought I was better off being by myself. The breakup of our engagement was hard on me, so I did what I knew best. I stayed focused on work. The breakup all but destroyed Robert, and he contemplated moving away to California with Anthony to get away and heal from this seemingly almost irreparable damage, little to my knowledge. I worked to push down my feelings so they wouldn't hurt me. I worked long hours to keep my mind forced on other things, and when I found myself thinking I made a mistake, I wanted Robert back in my life. I worked harder and longer hours to stay focused on moving forward with my life, but deep down inside, I knew he was the infamous "one." I didn't want to admit it, that stubborn bull raging inside of me. I didn't want to lose the person I fought to become. Did I even understand what I had forged my being into yet? Who was this woman I was clinging onto so hard? Was I ever meant to live a life by myself? Did I not deserve to live a life full of love and happiness and find a balance between both worlds?

Robert wasn't doing well at all. He stopped eating, and all his friends lashed at me for breaking his big yet fragile heart. The breakup felt like China glass shattering into a million broken pieces across the floor of his life.

Absolute devastation. After two months apart, I was driving my car back from a friend's house. As I pulled into my complex, Robert was standing at my car door. This totally scared the shit out of me, I might have even peed my pants a little. In a fit of rage, I yelled at him and said I was going to get a restraining order to keep him away from me. He pleaded to give him a chance and asked me to talk. I said no because I thought it was better if we weren't together. I was really stubborn, damn that bull inside me. Later that night, he stood outside of my bedroom window in the snow looking up. As I was getting ready for bed, I was pulling down my curtain and saw him, like a stranded puppy alone in the snow waiting for his owner to come to grab him. I opened the window told him to go to the gate, and I would let him in. His damn puppy face was just too adorable. He came into my apartment; my roommate had left so we could talk freely. We hugged, and he said, "Dawnmarie, I can't live without you"! I started to cry the next thing we were talking about everything that had happened after our breakup. I asked him to stay the night with me. After seeing him, I knew I was missing him in my life and that I still loved him.

Okay, so everybody has seen "The Notebook" by Nicholas Sparks, right? Well, we made love like never before that night. Rachel McAdams & Ryan Gosling have nothing on Robert, and I compared to their scene in the rain when Gosling's character states, "I did write all these years." We had snow, so beat that Nicolas Sparks. Where are my movie rights? It indeed was something better than any romance film. He told me he was moving to California. Because life without me was heartbreaking. And he needed to move on with his life in a new location. I asked when he said next week. I wanted to cry, but I didn't. I wanted him to know that I genuinely missed him. We spent every day together before he left for his new life without me in California. We had a week to remember, he took me to expensive dinners, took me shopping, brought me flowers, and we laughed like when we first met. We were living life again like before. I fell deeper in love with him all over again. How could I let him go? Life was great until the planning of the wedding and all the outside stresses reeled in. People were trying to tell us how to be and what to do, everyone was telling us we were moving too fast. I felt I was losing my self...it was Robert I was losing myself too.

Chapter 15 - The Pretty Woman Treatment

Goddamnit Richard Grier, I was living the real-life Pretty Women. This fairy tale with Robert continued, and he said he couldn't live without me, and that's why he was moving. All a ploy, unbeknownst to my knowledge to draw me in closer. Meanwhile, I didn't know what to do. I couldn't let him go, I knew we loved each other, and if it were meant to be, we would find a way back to each other. I had to let him go. These were confusing times. Before I knew it, he was leaving the next morning for his new life in California without me. I took him to the airport. I didn't want him to see me cry. It used everything I had in me to hold back all my tears and emotion as they called his flight number and said that they were boarding. He hugged and kissed me goodbye. I felt like I was losing a piece of my heart. As he walked down the runway, he turned and spoke in his powerful yet gentle voice, "you know where to find me." I couldn't look back, I wanted to, but I couldn't. I was torn apart from the inside out, and I didn't want him to see me like that. As I was driving home, my heart was being pulled apart, piece by lonely piece.

I knew at that very moment I couldn't live without him. When he arrived in California, he telephoned me. I told him that I loved him, and I couldn't live without him. I asked him to marry me. Now ladies, when you ask a man to marry you, you better hang up whatever it is you're doing whether it be drowning yourself in chocolate ice cream, watching that romantic flick that makes you flood your eyes with tears, or telephoning your girlfriends about your broken heart, you stop in your tracks and you chase that man down like you're a damn outlaw running away with the steal of a century. Robert was in tears over the phone and responded, "Yes, Dawnmarie, I will marry you." Before I knew it, he was back in Massachusetts, and we planned our wedding in two months.

We got married on September 2nd, 1990. We had the wedding of the century; it indeed was our fairy tale wedding. My wedding dress was made to fit me just like Cinderella's dress, but only more perfect. I wanted it to look classical, with the side of my dress full of tooling from the front. It looked absolutely majestic, and it trailed itself with seven feet long of material. My veil was hand made to fit my head, and Robert surprised me with an extra headpiece to add so it would cover my train of the wedding dress. We had over two-hundred, and fifty people attend our wedding. Family from both sides of our family came, and it was the biggest party of my life. Everything was black and white. The men all wore black tuxedoes, and my bridesmaids wore long silk gowns. They had silk tops with long black silk bottoms. We all had beautiful white roses to carry. My shoes had pure white silk flowers with diamond-like sparkles in them. After the ceremony, everyone danced for hours. Robert and I only danced once together, and that magical feeling of newly-weds was flooding the room the whole nite. We were so busy thanking everyone for coming from so far away, we barely had time for ourselves. We took all the photos you need when you get married, and before we knew it, our wedding night event was over. Looking back now, I am wishing we had danced the night away.

Chapter 16 - The Honeymoon

The very next day we left for our honeymoon, Robert planned for us to stay three weeks on our honeymoon in the Virgin Islands. It was so incredible and magical. We made love every day and had romantic dinners. Yes, we also went swimming and diving in the bluest water and took full advantage of the sun. Every day, we traveled all over the island in our rental Jeep. We would run into such a fantastic site and just pull to the side of the road to observe and inhale the beautiful tropical breeze and landscape. Everything was so simple there, life was good for the people who lived there, on multiple occasions we would spot an old man walking up a hill as he was hoarding a large group of sheep. On one of these occasions, Robert pulled the Jeep over to the side of this tiny dirt road. We got out of our car and approached the gentleman. Robert and I asked how long he had been working as a sheepherder? He smiled, with no teeth, and said this is my life and I love it. The sheep take care of me, and I take care of them. Then he told us about how he made cheese, milk, and all other kinds of products. He lived in a little shack down the road.

The sheep and the herder past by and Robert and I continued our drive. We kept stopping to look at all the incredible views I was experiencing for the first time. I could not stop taking pictures! I remember when we got to the bottom of this hill, we saw the gentlemen's shack and it was so adorable. We also saw the store down the dusty path, just as he said. Robert and I bought some food and then went down to the beach and had a picnic. After eating, we went swimming in the gleaming, crystal blue water. I turned around to find a goat right next to me, swimming in the ocean. I yelped at first then realized the goat was just hanging out. There were so many goats all over the island just hanging around and eating the grass; they were pretty much doing the same things Robert and I had scheduled. As I was walking out of the water, Robert took a picture of that goat and me. How amazing and entertaining that day was. We continued to explore the island and the village of little tourist shops. There where so many stores. We brought some things to bring home, and Robert brought me such a beautiful dress for dinner that night.

Robert had the hotel plan a dinner for two on the beach at sunset. It was so romantic. When we got back to our honeymoon suite, the bed had roses all over it with candles lighting up the room. Robert opened our doors to the outside of our suite, and then he played our wedding song. He asked me to dance, finishing our wedding dance that was all too waited for. I started to cry, immaculate tears of joy. Robert has always been romantic and a true gentleman; he is eloquent, compassionate, and most of all, he loves to write. It is as if I was Zelda Fitzgerald and Robert was F. Scott, he would pen onto his life with what he thought was the perfect story for us. Robert was composing his own Gatsby, and I was his Daisy. I was his muse, and he could write me into anything he could think of. We were so in love, and you could feel our love wherever we went.

No matter where we went, we both had the biggest smiles on our faces. Everyone kept asking us, "are you two on your honeymoon"? Of course, we said yes. We didn't want our honeymoon to end. I was so happy and so in love with Robert. This was our three weeks of pure bliss and romance. Every day a new adventure arose. From going on boat tours to all of the other islands around us to walked and exploring everything we could see around us, we truly made the best of our time. The sun was warm, the water was crystal blue, and magic was filling every glance with a dreamlike euphoria. For the first time in a long time, my phantoms' pains and Asthma never hindered my time on those islands. Life was truly amazing, and we were so in love I think you could see our happiness from miles away.

Chapter 17 - After the Honeymoon, And onto Real Life

Alas, our honeymoon ended, and we returned to normal life. Neither of us wanted it to end. We even tried to convince ourselves some nights to just stay and live the most uncomplicated life we could imagine there. However, Robert and I's dreams carried on beyond these tiny islands. We came home from our honeymoon and moved into our condominium. It was in an old converted warehouse that had exposed brick walls, rustic in styling, with twelve-foot ceilings. Our place was so charming. The fresh and new smell of the site had us excited to meet others in our complex. We even had a community pool for everyone who lived there. I started to work for a store called Macy's in their shoe department not long after we settled down. Robert didn't want me traveling anymore for work, so I took a manager's role instead of a district manager role. I liked it at first, but then I was bored with such a simple job I was used to. So, I decided to transfer sections and became a department manager for the men's line. I worked weekends, holidays, and a total of 48 hours a week. Back to the classics as they say.

Along with the newfound work, my symptoms resurrected after that period of relief and were getting worse. I now had pins and needles in both hands all the time. My left eye was always blurry, and fatigue ever settled right alongside it. Once again, I went to my family doctor. I explained to him that I had had the same phantom pains for years, and he directed his assistants to perform more blood work for the thousandth time.

Everything came back normal! The doctor said to me, "Dawnmarie, you are most likely just stressed out from returning to work, especially with the workload you carry. I am giving you Xanax to relax when you are having these feelings again". Again, the same results without any solutions. The doctor continued to reassure and relax me. He most likely saw the distressed look on my face; unfortunately, I'm not very good at hiding when I feel uncomfortable. He said, "don't worry, everything will be okay. You are young". At this point, I really started to believe I was becoming a hypochondriac. If the doctors couldn't figure out what was wrong with me, was it all merely just psychological pain I was inflicting on myself from all those years growing up in isolation?

Robert and I settled in, and life was calm for a while. When my pains would surface, I would take the pills as instructed to subside those terrible feelings. Robert and I began to talk about having children around this time, and before I knew it, I became pregnant. It's funny how life just throws you a curveball so early on in one's marriage. I was scared and very nervous. I thought something was going to happen, and that feeling was getting worse with each day. I wondered if our child-to-be would be like me. I would never want to inflict my pains from my childhood onto such an innocent and gentle life. I was terrified of the rotating doors coming to and from the hospital. I simply didn't want my child always to feel different as I did. I was totally stressed out. After six weeks, I miscarried our baby. The pain and emotional distress that followed was so hard on me. I reacted like any woman would respond to this awful event. Was there something wrong with me? Was I unable to have children due to my years of constant medication messing up my system? I continued to stress more, and all the phantom pains were getting worse. I thought if I worked more and stayed busy, I wouldn't think about it.

The next significant chapter soon arrived at Robert and I's doorstep. We were presented with an excellent opportunity to move to California. When Robert asked me about the move, I was so excited to have a new adventure. It was that adventurous spirit in me that I wanted to travel the world that I felt tugging deep down. We packed up everything we had, put it all in a big U-Haul, and hooked up my blue Honda civic. Did you guys forget about my blue baby girl? As we drove cross county from Connecticut to California, we got stuck in the middle of a huge snowstorm. We had to stay in a motel where all truckdrivers stay when they were on long trips. We were snowed in for three days. On snowy days growing up, I would always watch movies, eat junk food, and cuddle with my stuffed animals. This time wasn't so different; Robert was my cuddle partner by the fireplace, and lovemaking obviously ensued. Not too bad if you ask me.

After the snowstorm was over, we packed up and continued the road trip. Time ticked by, and we made it to New Mexico. I started to notice I was having problems again this time with my legs. They were so fatigued from merely sitting in a car. It felt like I just pushed the car up a huge hill. All I was doing was reading a book and sitting in the passenger's seat. I told Robert about it, and we both thought that it was strange. We pulled over to walk a little. When I stepped out of the truck, my left leg gave out on me. I thought to myself, "This is so strange." We got lunch and then hit the road again. We had been on the road for days; Robert did all the driving from the East Coast to the West Coast. Before we knew it, we only had 13 hours to before we got to California. Robert was tired, and so was I. We stayed in a small hotel and got some sleep. As the sun crept up from the east, we were on the road again.

Chapter 18 – California: Round 1

We finally made it to our new home in Newport Beach, California. I loved the development we lived in. This was going to be such a new and exciting place to live in. I started to work at Victoria's Secret as a store manager at Fashion Island, an outdoor shopping mall in Newport Beach. Life was going really well; Robert had his own business dealing in the new and exciting world of rising technology. I worked 45 to 50 hours a week. The company was great to work for, and my team was amazing. This is where I met my best friend, Jenna. We remain best friends to this day. She was the most beautiful woman I had ever seen. I mean, not only by her looks, her heart was pure and filled with seemingly endless love. We worked long hours together because she was also a store manager for another VS store down the road. We had so much fun together.

Our new life as a married couple was going so well. Then, the strange phantoms started happing again. I would be making a floor move late at night, and I began to feel the pins and needles all over my arms and feet. I started to notice that if I worked long hours with little sleep, the phantoms kept coming back. I remember telling Jenna about it. I confessed that I thought I was going crazy. I had been to so many doctors and had all the blood work imaginable, and they all said there was nothing wrong with me. So, she suggested going to see a doctor for my headaches, vision problems, and my neck pain. Maybe that could give me some light on what's wrong with an individual approach. With Jenna's advice, I made an appointment, and the optometrist said I had 20/20 vision. My neck, according to the doctor, was having spasms, so they gave me a medication called Flexeril to help keep my symptoms from getting worse. The medication didn't help. I continued to think, "if this is just me, then I have to live with all of these phantoms."

One day at work, I was talking with my team about moving some props and items around and noticed that a whole table of clothing was gone. Out of the corner of my eye, I saw two people with large garbage bags shoplifting from my store. I started to approach them, and they grabbed the bags and started to run. I ran after them and yelled to the team to call the police. As I was running in high heels, one of the lifters dropped the bag while the other one kept running. Suddenly, as I was approaching the discarded bag, I felt my legs pull out from under me, and I collapsed to the floor. The two lifters got away with the other large bag of merchandise. The mall security team came over to me to help me up and walk me back to the store.

I was shaking and couldn't really feel my feet and legs. The mall security sat me down and had a medical team check me out. It felt like I had been knocked down by a truck full of bricks. The phantom fatigue and the pain were so intense I started to cry. Robert rushed to my work and took me to the hospital. They said I just pulled a leg muscle. The very next day, I was in more pain than I had ever felt before. My legs were weak, and my body was so fatigued. The phantoms surged and attacked from every angle it seemed. I took the medication Flexural and popped a Xanax. I went to a specialist he said I had pulled my Sciatic nerve. He gave me some medication, and I was out of work for three weeks.

With the medication, I could walk without feeling like I was going to fall flat on my face. My left hand, however, was always going numb on me. My visions continued to give me trouble. The idea of me losing my mind was the most outstanding thought in my head. Over those three weeks of recovery, I attended therapy three times a week for my legs. I would tell my therapist all the symptoms were happening to me, and she looked at me like I was a hypochondriac. I almost thought she was right. I started to keep it all to myself. I pushed that unresolved thought as deep as I could.

I went back to work at Victoria's Secret and continued my job with my all to famous smile. After work, I would go home feeling so fatigued, every damn day. Robert would ask me how I was doing, and I would tell him I was okay. I didn't want him to worry, it was my problem. So, I dealt with the everyday pains that had no name. It was around this time I coined the name phantoms. I didn't want to be that wife that was always complaining, blaming my pain and worries on my persistent sickness. I stayed focused on my job and worked hard every day, just like all those days before. I made every day seem like everything was great. The only person I would tell my problems to be was Jenna. She always agreed there was something wrong, the doctors were obviously missing something. These symptoms shouldn't be considered normal for any person. Jenna and I would laugh a lot together. She got married on September 4th. She married her best friend Bob who also worked in retail. They looked like the perfect couple. Bob was a giant with dark hair, and Jenna was everyman's dream. Before we knew it, Robert and I had been living in Newport Beach for four years.

Chapter 19 - The Haunted House

Robert sold his company to another software company, and following his sale, we were moving to New York. We lived in this little town called Port Jefferson. We moved into a little house right across from a beautiful Catholic church. This house was perfectly charming. The house had a wraparound white porch with two rocking chairs next to the front door. It was a light baby blue color with white shutters. It sat on a small hill and had trees and flowers all over the front of the porch. There was also a graveyard in our backyard, where the church would bury the people who had passed away. I didn't think much about it at the time.

We unpacked and settled into a new house and adventure once again. There were only one bedroom and a guest room upstairs. I made that my closet. The funny part of this faux guest room was the location of the sink and toilet taking up so much room in this minimal space. The roof of the house was one side of this space, so thank goodness I am only five feet, two inches. If I were any taller, I would've hit my head every day just trying to get dressed for the day. I would have been the perfect fourth member of the Three Stooges. The full bathroom was downstairs to the side of the den. Robert's office was set up near that. It had an old bathtub with a crawl-feet. In the corner was a makeshift shower with a shower curtain alongside the sink that was original to the home.

The floors in the house were all original as well, except the kitchen floor; it was tile. After settling into our home, Robert and I started to get to know the small town and all the roads. Soon after that, I started working right away. I would drive into the Big City every day. I transferred from my current job at Victoria's Secret in California to another of Victoria's Secret in New York. I was a store manager once again. My team was amazing, and the store was doing so well. The one thing that was always a hassle on me was the drive. The traffic in NYC Is like a personal hell for anybody who drives those roads. Somedays, I would listen to books on tape. This made my drive much easier for me. I did love seeing all the changes in the weather again in California. We had differences of climate, but nothing like the East coast; this was refreshing to me at first. From seeing the first rusted leaf fall to the first glistening of snow, and the shimmering of rain during the early Spring, The East Coast always was full of pleasant change.

On most days after work, I would drive home, and the weather was pretty normal since the time Robert, and I moved in. However, there will always be one drive home that I always will remember. It was a rainy day, so the traffic was backed up to the city edges. It was insane; even as my car crawled its way home, the wind was thrashing and blowing my car all over the road. I was driving a Honda Accord at the time; it was dark green and had a tan interior. I've always had cars with colors that would cheer me up, especially when I was stressed out. When I look at brightly colored vehicles, my mood increases a thousand percent or some ridiculous number like that. Anyways, "that" night I got home; the entire sky was like something out of a horror film. The rain was falling, the wind was blowing waves of fury, and I was terrified. Every noise that I heard scared the living hell out of me. I was walking up the stairs to the front door of my home. Lighting struck the tree directly across the street. That scared the shit out of me, and I ran into the house. As I stumbled inside, I found the power was out because the lights obviously weren't working. This sounds like I'm about to be set-up like any victim in a horror flick, right? Just wait. I went into the kitchen and looked for the flashlight, so I could see where I was going. I found it and then pulled out some candles. I proceeded to light them and put one in the living room, one in the den, and one in the kitchen.

The house felt cold and desolate of life. Robert was on his way home from a long week of working in Boston. To make matters slower, he drove instead of flying. I was definitely going to be "Friday the 13th'ed" now. I called him when he was on the ferry coming back from Boston to Port Jefferson and told him the storm was terrible. As I tried to hold back my terror, I spoke into the phone saying Robert, "The wind and trees are swinging all over, a-a-and we don't have electricity. I'm kind of scared". Knowing very well, I was absolutely petrified. The house was super creepy and was making lots of unnerving noises. Every room in the house seemed unfriendly and emotionless. I remember sitting in the living room and thinking to myself this house is definitely haunted.

As I sat there, my thoughts imagining the most horrific endings imaginable, Robert arrived home in two hours after our call. I was so happy he was back with me. I told him the house was haunted; he laughed and said I was letting my imagination run wild. I felt much calmer with Robert in the house. We talked about our work week, and we were both exhausted, so we went to bed. In the middle of the night, as Robert and I were sleeping, I heard someone at the front door screaming let me in. Again, this scared the shit out of me. I could not get any relief it seemed. Robert confronted the man at the door and told him to leave. The man refused to go, so we had to call the police. The very next day, Robert called the local alarm company to come out and install a security system in the house. I was praying this would make me feel better.

Robert traveled all the time, and I was commuting back and forth to work. I drove over four hours each day to work and home. This alone was so stressful. Work made me happy and gave me purpose. I truly loved my job and being surrounded by beautiful things all day made it all the better for yours truly. How could one not be happy? I was working with women and selling them sexy lingerie to make them feel confident and beautiful. That was the essence of Victoria's Secret, and I loved every minute of my job. The women I worked with daily all had each other's back. It was long hours and weekends, but it kept me busy and entertained. So, on my days off, I started to explore the town. It was like going back in time. All the houses were old, and so were all the cities around us. I would visit the little shops and walk around the small villages in Stony Brook. The name of the small town we lived in was, Port Jefferson. It was an incorporated village in the town of Brookhaven in Suffix County, New York on the north shore of Long Island. Officially known as the Village of Port Jefferson the population was 7,750. Port

Jefferson was first settled in the 17th Century, so this small town had some deep history, and so did our house.

When Robert was out of town on business, I didn't like being in the house by myself. Some of you reading this part of my story may think, "wow! She really is crazy", I wouldn't blame yourself for thinking such things. I would hear noises all the time, like someone walking up and down the stairs and hallway, even when I was the only one in the house. Every room was always super cold even with the heat on blast. This house gave me the jeepers creepers. When we moved into the house, there were so many locks on every door of our home. We both thought this was crazy; there were five kinds of locks on every door, and the windows were all old as well. The only remodel the house had even been through was the kitchen. It had one of those old scary basements like Norman Bate's house. Don't even get me started on the creeks and noises while going down the stairs. They were old and spaced far between one another. Every time I had to go downstairs, the movie "Carrie" by Brian De Palma would play in my head, and I could imagine a hand coming up and grabbing me. On the first day moving into the house, I moved some boxes of Christmas stuff down to the basement. It had a dirt floor, but it was the ground itself. The bricks stacked underneath were holding up the house, so we couldn't even get rid of it.

I really hated this basement when I was down there; I seriously thought to myself that I could feel negative energy all around me. Not only was the basement freezing all the time, but I would hear weird noises behind the stairwell. When Robert traveled, I never wanted to go home because the house really scared me, I always felt like someone was watching me. I was having all the phantom pains all over my body and continued to think I was going crazy. So, to make me feel more comfortable at home, we decided to get a German Shepard. We named him Zeus after the Greek god of Olympus. He was so adorable and fluffy. He was colored black and light tan and was a bucket full of energy. We took him to puppy training classes in town. Robert did most of the training because Zeus listened to him more than me. I still totally loved having him around me, even when he was a little brat, his warmth and playfulness made me feel safe. Zeus was like a fluffier and smaller Robert. Every day, when I would leave for work, Zeus would stay in the kitchen. We put up a puppy gate for him so he could roam a little bit without feeling too cramped. The funny thing was that Zeus would always bark at the basement door and the hallway adjacent to Robert's office.

When Robert was gone on overnight trips, Zeus would sleep in the bed with me. I remember one night when Zeus stood at the entrance to the hallway and growled as his hair was standing up across his back; he was in full protection mode because obviously, something was there lurking in the dark. I knew there was something wrong in this house, and I could feel every inch of it. I had always had a good sense of understanding the waves of energy emitted by my surroundings and the people I surround myself near even when I was a little girl. I could feel when someone was a bad or good person, call it a gut feeling. I have always relied on this throughout my entire life, and I'm pretty sure I'm 98% right all the time. I know that something terrible happened in this house.

There was a day when I had two days off from work. I remember taking Zeus for a walk up the hill behind my house. The graveyard for the church was also located there. Zeus didn't like it there, and I didn't either; before I knew it, Zeus took off I couldn't hold the leash. He went running down the street, and I chased after him. My legs felt so weak, and they came out from under me. I fell and started to cry. I had scratches all over my legs and hips. Thankfully, someone up the street saw me fall and went after Zeus and brought him back to me. We went back home, and I cleaned up all the cuts all over my legs. I took some Tylenol and laid down. I called Robert and told him what had happened. We laughed on the phone together, even though the stinging pain. He could always make me laugh. I really missed Robert every time he would have to travel, at least I had Zeus to keep me company. Although I had Zeus with me, I remember I was playing with him after work one night, and he started to bark at the staircase again. This sent an immediate red flag down through my body. I was shaking in fear, as I imagined a grotesque face staring at me, even though nothing was there.

Robert would laugh at me every time I told him my stories; except they weren't just stories. There was one day after coming home from work, Zeus was going crazy. He was barking at nothing; well, nothing I could see at least. He ran to me rapidly, like he was protecting me from someone. I said to him, "Zeus, it's ok darling," and began to pet him to calm him down. I got his ball and thought he would chase after it but stopped suddenly as the ball rolled down the hallway. Zeus started barking again, and his hair stood up on his back like sharp blades. Then suddenly, the ball came rolling back down the hallway by itself. Now, I know what you're thinking, and yes, I might have peed myself a little at this point. There was a step in the middle of the hallway, so there was no way the ball could roll back without hopping a few steps backward. It was Zeus and me, alone, in the devil's residence. I was trembling, like rocks falling from a cliff, and it felt like I was going to shit myself; I didn't. I called

Zeus to come to me, but he wouldn't stop barking in the hallway. There was something in the house, and it wasn't an entity I wanted to be around. It was malevolent, and Zeus could see it. I reached for Zeus with great hesitation and pulled him into the living room. I was so scared; I thought, "shit!", something is going to appear from the hallway, and I am going to scream in terror. I made Zeus sit next to me on the couch until Robert got home.

Robert doesn't believe in "GHOSTS." Robert's brother, Donald, did though. So, Donald moved in with us, while he was searching for some new work. This made things easier on me, and he loved Zeus. Donald would take care of him in the long days when I was working. If Robert was out of town, I had a company to talk to as well. I remember one night we were watching TV and Zeus started barking at the stairwell. I asked Donald if he thought the house was haunted? After all the stories I shared with him, Donald concurred that there was something haunted about this house. He too could feel specific energies around himself, so he was just as sensitive to the changes in the house as I. Validation at last! I would talk to Donald about my anxiety and nervousness when I was in the house alone. He was the brother I had always wanted and understood where I was deriving my feelings from. We talked about the phantoms haunting me since I was a late teenager and reassured me that I was not going crazy. Like Jenna, he suspected the doctors were missing something. This helped my confidence out a lot. I was being assaulted internally by my own phantoms and externally by whatever was in the house.

Robert's mother, Judith, came for a visit one weekend from Massachusetts. She thought the house was cute but also had strange feelings when stepping inside. The three of us, myself, Donald, and Judith all thought the house was haunted. It was built in the early 1800s and was located next to a damn graveyard. Who knows what could have happened in the house or near the property? For all I knew, the house could be sitting on ancient native American burial grounds. I remember going to the library and looking up deaths in our home. It said that people have passed away in the house, but I couldn't find anything about any murders in the house. That doesn't mean it didn't happen.

Chapter 20 – Boston, Our Next Chapter

Well, we lived in that house for 10 months, and Victoria's Secret asked me to transfer to Boston, Massachusetts, thank god! Without hesitation, I said yes. I hadn't even consulted with Robert yet, all I knew was, I wanted out of that damn house, and I didn't want to make the drive to work anymore. The latter is the real reason, let's be honest here. When I told Robert about my decision, we went to Boston to look for a new home. We bought a beautiful condo right on the water with views overlooking Quincy, Massachusetts. The day rolled around when it was time to move out of that wretched New York home, and I told Robert and Donald that I will wait in the car with Zeus, out of reach from whatever was in there. Robert's dad, Donald, came down to help pack up the house. I didn't even care if they left everything behind, I simply wanted to get the hell out of that house. Robert's cousin, Cherly, had a condo in Boston that I stayed at until all the paperwork was finished from buying the condominium.

Our new condo was close to my new job. It was totally adorable and had a full alarm system, including security at the front door. I felt safe being there by myself. Unfortunately, we moved Zeus into Robert's mothers' house. I was without my guard dog, but my feelings for safety remained. I remember I worked a double shift one day, so I got back to the condo later that night. I took a shower, talked to Robert on the phone, and headed for bed. I was sound asleep, and suddenly, I started to hear voices in the condo. My mind began racing, and all I could think of was, "dammit, here we go again." I tried to make sense of the noise because I knew Cherly wasn't in town and thought I was just hearing things. Then I heard a man's voice talking to another man; I got up out of bed and opened the bedroom door, and three huge black men were standing in her living room. For some reason, I didn't feel scared or afraid. I said, "hello, who are you?", and they replied, "who are you?" I said, "I am Cheryl's cousin through marriage." They said Cheryl had given them keys and were always allowed to stay at her place when they were in town. In response, I called Cheryl, and she notified them that they were not allowed to stay at the condo while I was living there. One of them knocked on my bedroom door and apologized for the intrusion. They proceeded to leave afterward, and I called Robert next and told him.

The very next day, I went to work, and all three of the men showed up with a dozen red roses to apologize for scaring me. I said, "you didn't scare me at all," and laughing ensued. As time went on, they all continued to visit me at work, and we all became good friends.

The new VS location seemed to fit me well, and like all the times before, I loved the team I was working with. I continued to work the regular retail routine and took it for what it was, but at least I was a manager. On the positive side, everything was going so well for Robert and me. Not everything is flowers and rainbows, and I started to experience strange symptoms in my stomach. I began to feel an unnerving pain in my abdomen like I had someone stabbing me in my uterus. I would have my regular menstrual cycles, but they became increasingly painful and would last for weeks. I decided to make an

appointment with my gynecologist, Dr. David. At the'
doctor's, they ran a variety of tests and found I had
endometriosis. Endometriosis can be a painful disorder
because the tissue that should be inside of the uterus
lining grows on the exterior of the uterus instead. I was
scheduled and put under for surgery to clean out all the
excess scar tissue. I had a checkup two days post-surgery
when the doctor asked me how I was doing?
I replied stating I had so much more pain than before the
surgery. It felt like I had a blow torch burning me from
inside. I remember him looking at me like I was crazy,
and he said I shouldn't be feeling any more pain. I broke
down in tears and looked at him. I yelled, "I am not
crazy! And this pain shouldn't be worse than before this
damn surgery"! In response, he gave me some pain
medication and sent me on my way. I would take the
medication and work at the same time, but the phantom
pains continued to enthrall me. The pain was almost
unbearable, and I took everything in me to just get
through the day. But I still went back to work put a smile

on my face and barreled through it. Yes, you can call me Wonder Woman.

I would get home from work, and all I would want to do was take my medication and pass out. On top of the excruciating pain I was feeling when I was just by myself, I was also experiencing pain during intercourse. I simply wanted to be close to my husband, and I couldn't even experience this pleasure without the agony. Talk about paradoxical. I didn't want to upset Robert, because I felt if I kept complaining he would get tired of hearing me do so. I worried he might want to look elsewhere. The emotional distress was increasingly persistent around this time; I was a wreck. One of my greatest fears was Robert leaving me for another woman; a woman who didn't have problems.

The phantoms were wrapping their clutch around my whole life, and I had zero answers to counteract their assault. I was stressing out all the time and living in more pain than ever before. Pins and needles inflamed my extremities, following extreme fatigue, headaches, and severe vertigo. I started to believe I was going crazy, the fear of this reality becoming normal scared the living hell out of me. How could this keep happing to me? Again, I decided to go to a family doctor located in Boston. They basically gave me a general physical and ran a series of blood work. At my follow up appointment, they said that I was overly stressed, and all my blood work indicated all systems appeared normal. The doctor spoke to me, "Dawnmarie, you look healthy and good. You simply are over-working yourself and need to rest. I'm going to prescribe you some medication called Xanax". This was the standard medication doctors gave out to all females to reduce stress and pain.

I remember talking to my girlfriends about my situation and the continuing frustration I was facing with the continuous doctors' visits. Every time I would go to the doctors, I would wait for over an hour in their offices before even seeing a doctor. Finally, when I was able to see the doc, I would be in their office for 5 minutes, and they would write a perception and send me on my way. I was thinking to myself that I should have become a doctor because every doctor I had seen over the years always said the same thing. There had to be some secret script every doctor followed, I thought to myself. They never seem to care, and they dismissed me all the time without even addressing any of my issues. If I was a man, I believe they would have taken more time to address all my concerns, but this is my opinion. Time continued to drift away, and the pain continued. Before I knew it, Robert and I were moving again...

Chapter 21 - The Move to Findlay Ohio

Robert had a fantastic opportunity that would take him far in his career, but it required us to move to Findlay, Ohio. Yep, you heard that correctly, I said Findlay Ohio. We sold our condominium and bought a lovely, quaint, brick house with four thousand square footage and one acre of land. The house was huge for just the two of us, it looked like we needed to expand our family.

I loved it there, and I was even able to start a new job with Victoria's Secret. They transferred me to Ohio with ease. I stayed with the company for another six months before I transitioned to become a district sales manager for Paul Harris Clothing. The district I ran stretched from Columbus, Ohio to Detroit, Michigan. This was a fresh new start for me. An assortment of new stores and new people captured me with joy. I was also making a lot more money, and they even gave me a company car! It was not baby blue though; I was a tiny bit sad about that.

I was traveling a lot by car from one location to the next and had a lot of overnight stays in hotels. I loved my job, but something was missing. Robert and I wanted to have children; we had been married for six years and thought it was time. I became pregnant, and we were both so excited. At 4 weeks, we went to our OBGYN, Dr. Wingate; he was the most caring doctor I had ever encountered. Things were looking good, he said, and I continued to work. Robert was working and traveling all the time, as well. He would travel from the Midwest to the west coast and back to the east coast. He practically ran a country at this point. On my days off, I was home by myself, and the work I brought home kept me super busy. Eight weeks into the pregnancy, I started spotting blood, and this scared me. Robert was in town working, thankfully, in his office at Solomon Software. I called him, and then he called our doctor. They had me brought into the office and did an ultrasound. Dr. Wingate's response was some of the most terrible news I will ever hear in my life, "I'm sorry Robert and Dawnmarie, but the baby doesn't have a heartbeat." I had lost the baby.

Unfortunately, women experience this kind of pain every day when it comes to pregnancy. The fear of losing their pregnant child is haunting; It feels like you lose a genuine part of yourself when you lose a child. I looked at Robert, and I cried and cried and cried; Robert broke down with me. Our tears flooded the room. As we tried to piece ourselves back together, we told Dr. Wingate about all the phantom pains I had been experiencing over the years. We asked if these were one of the reasons I miscarried. He replied and said, "This could be a possibility, but I don't know for sure. I have never heard about someone experiencing these symptoms simultaneously". Wingate asked what my previous doctors told me about my prognosis, and I said, "From all my visits, the doctors repeatedly told me I was a completely healthy human being, and my blood work indicated nothing was abnormal." Wingate responded, "I think you might be too young to carry a child and you shouldn't worry too much right now. The time will come". On the drive home, I didn't say anything, I sat there lifeless; I had lost a part of myself, and Robert could feel it. Thoughts bombarded my brain, and I feared I would never be able to bear a child! I started working again, and I continued to perform excellently as always. I did anything I could to get my mind off losing our child. My work rewarded me by giving me even more stores to manage. At least I was able to do something correctly. Working hard had always put a smile on my face, but it was getting harder and harder each day. My physical and emotional pains continued to enthrall my life. When I wasn't working, my thoughts traveled to the darkest locations. They lurked there like a predator waiting for its prey.

I would be home alone in this empty house and think to myself these rooms would never be filled with the laughter and happiness a child brings to one's life. My depression and physical pains continued to strike. My visions continuously faltered along with the broken feeling of numbness along my left side. I continued to think that this was a waking dream, and I would wake up, and everything would be alright; this, unfortunately, was my reality. I tried to stay positive and keep a smile on my face, but my mask was beginning to form around my disfigured little world. As the old idiom goes, "fake it, until you make it." I tried to make new friends and work a lot, but deep down the pain strangled my entire being. I was popping the Xanax a lot now to escape; it probably was way too much. I went to my family doctor, and he administered another prescription. I asked him to listen to me so I could explain how misplaced my mind had become. He told me to write it all down for another time and make another appointment. The dismission fractured my already shattered reality.

Chapter 22 – My Reality Rewritten

I continued to keep my mind focused on work, and every day, I would try to convince myself, "all will be good." Thank god I was instilled with the inherent human trait to hope for a better future. Albeit, it was getting harder and harder each day to look for that dimming light.

My thoughts had broken through my reality, and I realized I was... crazy. How can the dominoes of my life keep tumbling, when my whole life I have been resilient? I was a young, hard-working wife, and I excelled at my job and my marriage. My reality was so fractured that I almost believed these symptoms, pains, and thoughts were my "normal." A crazy idea appeared in my head; maybe a sprit was haunting my entire existence? I went to my local church and attended confession. I told the father everything about my life from my depression to the miscarriages. His smile reassured me and rekindled that dimming flame of hope I was clinging onto so desperately. We said prayers, and he reassured me that I didn't have any evil spirits inhabiting my life. He could feel and see that I was a good person. He blessed me with holy water and gave me prayers to say when I felt depressed and alone. He told me to recite their prayers when I felt like I was losing control over my body. He also gave me a rosary that he blessed in front of me. That day rekindled a light in me that I had almost all but forgot about. He told me when I was stressed and alone to come to church. The church would always be a dock for me to tie my sailing mind to when I was lost at sea. Life went on, and my reality began to rewrite itself slowly. Even with the phantoms still lurking in the shadows, I took myself to the place where I knew I was comfortable so the healing would continue. Work was taking off again, and I was promoted. Work was one consistent tenant that helped me keep it all together. Robert and I decided to go on vacation to California in Newport Beach, where we lived when we first got married. We had a fantastic holiday. The relaxation and romance ignited the air around us, and I loved every minute of our escape. The sun was warm and calming as we relaxed with sand between our toes. We had dinners out and went to the beach almost every day; our drives up and down Pacific Coast Highway reassured me that life was a rollercoaster, and I could see a high on the horizon.

After vacation, our life went back to normal in Findlay, Ohio. Robert worked long hours, and so did I. I traveled all over the Midwest and focused on my job. Four weeks after our return, I realized I didn't have a menstrual cycle. So, I went to CVS and bought a pregnancy test. I went to the little girls' room and peed on the small stick. As I waited nervously for the result, I looked down, and it indicated I was pregnant. I exited the restroom and bought another one to make sure; it was positive again. When Robert got home, I showed him the two tests, and we exploded with joy after such a difficult couple of months. I made an appointment with Dr. Wingate again, and they tested me to make sure the diagnosis was correct. The test came back positive, and Wingate said we were going to have a baby. He said to both of us that things would work out this time.

I had my check-up at six weeks, and things were going well. I continued to work and travel, but I was so tired all the time. The phantoms began to inflict more damage once again in the shadows. I thought to myself, if every doctor had previously stated that nothing was wrong with me, then I guess this is just my normal. Right?

Our eight-week check-up rolled around again. Dr. Wingate performed another ultrasound, and without any indication before our check-up, Wingate broke some unbearable news once again. My child was without a heartbeat...

My body quaked, like never before. My tears filled my face as I gasped for air. My throat clenched, and my breath shuttered without a single noise forming. I looked at Robert, and he was trying to hold it back, but our shared pain was too much for even the strongest man I knew. He hugged me, and our clothing was leeched together by the boiling water pouring from our faces. Was this what hell felt like? To be wrought with despair and pain in the most unimaginable way possible? As Wingate looked down at us, he tried to reassure us that we would be able to have a child one day; One day, one day, one goddamn day! Those words rang through my mind, but it was incapable of grasping onto the concept. My fate was inescapable, I would be childless for the rest of my life. Fear, anger, and depression seeped through my being, and I wanted to yell at the sky, asking why I was cursed? Robert and I simply wanted to build a family, but that hope was being dragged away with each longing moment. After three tries, I was ready to give up.

When we got home, all I could do was cry. I called in sick that next day. I told my boss I needed some time off and that I had lost my baby again. Patty, my Boss, was so sweet to me and said take as much time as you need; God bless her soul. I remember taking a walk along the riverbank behind our house, and I sat down in the leaves and started weeping. As I wept and wallowed, my reality had been entirely unwritten. Was my existence worth all this pain and unwanted chaos? I can't even carry a child, without my feeble mind and body killing it from the inside out. No doctor, from East to West, could even tell me why all of this is happing to me. The distress pointed to one solution; how could I take my life?

Chapter 23 – Contemplation & Continuing Trials

I went home and thought to myself that Robert didn't need this in his life. I was distraught, and I couldn't even be a good wife and give him the thing he wants most in life, a family. The phantoms wouldn't let me carry a child, or was it secretly my mind telling me I couldn't? Taking my life, was the only streamlined decision that I felt would not only end my pain but Robert's pain as well. Suicide, this word has been prevalent throughout my life. I'm sure most of you are reading this book have even imagined it before, and possibly taken steps to fulfill those thoughts. Trust me, it seems simple at first; you could take those pills and fall asleep and never wake up. Most people are afraid to open up and talk about all of it and let me tell you I have been there. I have been the one to shut out every single person surrounding me, and I have been selfish to think that if I ended it all, my pain and everyone else's would end. It is not that simple. My life, just like yours, is a delicate string of webs interconnecting us and all we are to every single being we have ever touched. We are mostly all unaware of these thoughts until we actually face the decision of ending our life. When you sever yourself from the world around you and take those steps toward ending it all, the thoughts that flood your brain are sometimes the only things keeping you afloat. The connections one makes with another person or place throughout your life tether's your mind and soul to the world, and when it disconnects, it sends a ripple to all those connections because you're no longer there.

So, this was me. Here at the end of the line, it seemed, struggling to continue my existence. The scary thing was since I was so young, I wasn't conceptualizing what I just previously stated. I was so selfish to think that I could end it all, and the world would be unbothered. How could I believe that Robert could move on with his life and not live without me? I made a call to my girlfriend Jenna, remember my best friend from California, and told her I lost another baby. Jenna said it happens and to hang in there. Everything will work out when the time is right. Everything will work out when the time was right. Everything would work out when the time WAS right.

Ha, it didn't seem like it; that was the farthest I have ever felt from my reality. As I continued to listen to Jenna, the haze blocked most of her words, but she asked me, "Dawnmarie, have you been to any new doctors and spoken about the crazy thing that keeps happening to you?" I replied, "no, because they keep telling me the same goddamn thing"! Jenna told me to pray and stay calm. She said to me in the most compassionate voice I had ever heard, "Dawnmarie, life is going to hit you with everything it has holstered sometimes, but you are one of the most hopeful and strongest women I know. Your light helps drive even my own". Her words pulled on something that I had thought long gone by this point, the heartstring of hope. She finished by letting me know she was praying for me. I said thank you and told her that I loved her and missed her so much. I remembered all those crazy times we had in California and that heartstring continued to pull inside me, albeit it was a tiny kick, but it was there. As I hung up the phone, I felt reassurance that life could rewrite itself once again, but for the better. I reminded myself to remain focused on the positive. I began to reimagine all the great things that I had tethered myself to since I was just a little girl, and that helped me push on forward. This was merely a surface call.

Deep down inside, I was so frustrated, scared, and depressed. As I slowly returned to work, I acted like everything was perfect. I never showed all the pain I bundled inside myself. Xanax, that cursed medication. As much I wanted to take it all the time, I only administered the proper amount to elicit some sense of security in a world riddled with pain. The world was a consistent haze of pain-blocking. If I were on the road working, I would go out to dinner and have a glass of Zinfandel to shy myself, and then I would go back to my hotel. I would cry myself to sleep and wake up the next day, wondering why I was chosen to bear this pain? I put on my makeup, got dressed, and did my job again, and again, and again. Life became a pattern, devoid of excitement or pleasure. At the end of every day, I would collapse from exhaustion. I reached for anything to make me feel somewhere else, whether it be taking more Xanax,

Tylenol, Advil, or a glass of wine. This was my every day, dealing with all my phantom pain.

It was the only way I knew how to get through the days. Time passes, Robert and I kept trying to have a baby; no luck. I kept thinking to myself, if I can keep Robert happy by continuing to try, maybe he would still be able to love me. I stopped taking all the painkillers and went cold turkey. This was so hard, but how could I ever have a baby with all these chemicals in my blood. I struggled with chronic pain, and I began to pray every day. I asked for help from the one above. I asked him to help me be healthy, I asked him to help me be a good wife, and I asked him if I was a good person? I prayed a lot. I went to see another doctor, Dr. Weights, and he told me to keep track of my menstrual cycle. Every fourteen days, after having my period, I would be ovulating. I prayed and stayed focused on the good things my life. It took everything I had to try to have a baby.

I began ovulating one week, but I was all the way in Detroit, Michigan, working for the week. I called Robert, and he drove four hours so we could try and get myself pregnant again. Then he drove all the way home the same night because he had a business to do in the morning in Findlay. I continued to work and travel, and before I knew it had been five weeks later. We went in to see Dr. Wingate again so he could run another pregnancy test; it was positive. This time I said I wasn't going to get excited because I could lose another baby. It was so hard on me living in fear of losing another child that I didn't even want to tell anyone about my new pregnancy. Robert, I, and the doctor were the only ones to know about this pregnancy. I carried this baby all the way until 12 weeks, and I thought to myself, "Ok, I think I can get excited now." I started to show this adorable little belly, so we told everyone we were having a baby. I even began to buy baby things, and we started looking at cribs, rocking chairs, and I also had to get new pregnancy clothing. We made our follow up appointment for an ultrasound, and we were so excited to see the baby. We were going to learn the sex of this baby this time. Robert was with me for this appointment, and he was excited as well, he gripped my hand so firmly it was comforting and hopeful. The nurse took us into to ultrasound room and got me ready. Dr. Wingates came in and begun the ultrasound. We could see a baby, but it wasn't moving. I asked if the baby was sleeping; the doctor didn't even whisper a word. He turned the sound up and moved the wand around some more and looked at me. With great hesitation, he spoke, "I don't hear a heartbeat." I was speechless, my throat clenched on itself again and I couldn't even voice a whimper. Instead, I turned to Robert; he looked at me, and the tears had already welled up around his eyes, and he said, "I am so sorry." I started to cry, and Robert came over to hug me, and he held my hand as he always had. Wingates left the room, and we both cried together. This was the longest I had ever carried a baby. Hopelessness wasn't even a word I could use to describe how I felt. I was living in a world desolate of happiness, and my mask couldn't be held up any longer.

Soon after we tried again, out of pure desperation. At sixteen weeks, I miscarried again. This time, since the fetus had grown so large within me, they had to do a

DNC on me. I watched as the doctors pulled this lifeless being, that was supposed to be my child, from inside me. The physical pain was so excruciating that my torment stretched all the way to the depths of my own personal hell. Leaving the hospital, I felt lost. Was there anywhere left for me to go? I had been pregnant five times and miscarried all of them.

Chapter 24 - Lost & Alone

I knew Robert was having a hard time with this just like me, but he didn't show me. He was dealing with our loss the only way he could, he worked a lot. I stopped answering the phone because I couldn't even take one more, "I am sorry for your loss." I know everyone cared about Robert and me, but I just couldn't handle it. I wept for what felt like years. One day about five weeks after losing our fifth baby, I sat down with Robert. In a shaken and trembling voice, I said, "Robert, I'm worthless. I can't even give you the love you need because I don't even love myself. I can't give you the family you have wanted your entire life. I think we should talk about splitting up." He replied firmly, "Dawnmarie, I love you to the ends of the earth. No matter what we face together, on the day I married you I promised that for better or for worse I would be there standing by your side. I love you, and there are other options. We could adopt and start a family from there". Divorce was not an option, and to this day, he has stuck with for better or for worse.

Time passed; we both worked all the time, hardly ever seeing each other. I was on the road all the time with my job trying to hide my pain by still putting on a smile for the world, but when I was alone in my hotel room, I would cry nonstop. I would always think of taking my life. I was falling deeper and deeper into the black hole of pain and torment. I was afraid to tell Robert I was in so much pain from the phantoms of pain, that I held them in, and they thrashed inside my body, tearing me apart, piece by bloody piece. It had no name and no matter what kind of doctor I went to, they never had answers I sought to hear. I should just commit myself to an asylum at this point and further my loneliness. When we were together, I would put on a smile and pretend everything was okay. He knew I wasn't healthy or in a positive place; We just didn't know what to do or say. We were both lost.

Soon after the horrible events unfolded, I got a phone call from Dr. Wingate to come into his office. So, Robert and I went to visit him, and after waiting for what felt like centuries, we were finally in his room. Wingates suggested we perform full-scale DNA testing on both of us to see if that was the problem. The problem was my ability to carry a child. Robert and I completed all the tests per the doctor's request, and after 2 weeks of waiting for the results, we finally got the call to revisit Wingate's in his office. At the office, the three of us went through all the test results. Everything was good! Robert was perfect in balance, and all my results indicated I should be able to carry a baby. I was not sure how to feel happy or sad, then I told Dr. Wingate's about how my depression was affecting my ability to reason and handle everything. Wingates reassured me that all the symptoms I was feeling, the despair, self-hate, and loneliness were all products of the back-to-back pregnancies and all the ugly hormones that come with it. No wonder I was such a wreck. My body had been through so much over my entire life, and carrying a baby makes one's body go into more whacky and weird shapes, no wonder everything I was going through felt like it was being piled on top of me. The doctor suggested I go on more Xanax to help with the rollercoaster of emotions I was experiencing.

I began to take the higher dosage of my prescription, and when nighttime rolled around, it was time for me to relax and go to sleep. The Xanax made it easier to sleep, but who said anything about stopping nightmares? I would wake up having nightmares almost every night I took my prescription. At this point, I was working over 70 hours a week and traveling so much. My schedule was my only secure activity in my life; I knew I could trust that. Robert continued to travel a lot as well, so the loneliness remained. We had given Zeus away to Robert's mother so she would feel more comfortable at home, so I was genuinely alone without Robert. We only saw each other maybe two times a week. We were committed to each other, and divorce wasn't an option by any means.

It was a Saturday morning, much like any other, and we were both homes. I said we needed to talk, so went and sat on the back deck of our home. We talked about everything that had happened since we were together, and Robert began to talk about our future together. See, the future has always scared me; it is a path of uncertainty in the simplest of terms, and that scares the shit out of me. I looked at Robert and said something needed to change, no, I wasn't talking about us staying together, but I was talking about the life we were living together. We both looked at each other, and Robert said, "it's just you and me baby." From that point on, we both didn't talk about babies anymore. We would refrain from putting more stress on myself by avoiding the topic altogether. In the wake of our profound discussion, Robert booked a trip to Jamaica. We exposed ourselves to brilliant sunlight and fun for 2 weeks; it was a blast! I acquired one of the nicest tans of my life during our stay there. Our relaxation levels had reached an all-time high, and all the difficulties we had been having seemed to wash away with each passing tide. It was indeed something magical. While staying at our resort, we met some lovely new friends, who lived on the east coast as well. We even began to make plans for the four of us to travel together. The trip came to an end, as all good things do, and we returned to normal life. My normal life had seemed to change for the better, and this vacation helped push my more positive feelings towards the surface.

Chapter 25 – The "NEW" Roommate & Outlook

Robert's brother Donald moved into the house with us soon after our return from Jamaica. Donald was offered a job, by Robert, to work at the same company Robert was contracted to, Solomon. Donald gave me company when Robert was out of town, and our friendship grew. Like I said before, he is the brother I wish I had growing up. They both worked a lot of hours, and I did as well, and I began to construct Robert and I's future in my head. He and I were going to be husband and wife, with no children, busy careers, and traveling around the world. We had a big house with no children, so we had plenty of room for Donald to continue living with us. When Robert was out of town, Donald was there to keep me company. He was also engaged at the time, so his fiancée would be at the house sometimes. Our trio was cementing itself, but thoughts of bearing a child always remained deep in the back of my mind.

The one thing that always bothered me was everyone in our neighborhood had kids. When I would come home from work, all I would see were kids playing in the street and their yards while all the moms were hanging out. I couldn't help but feel I should be in that motherly circle. We had good neighbors, and all their kids were so adorable and sweet; I loved to see and play with them. I really enjoyed our neighborhood, we would talk to all our friends, and everyone got together pretty much every weekend. I was surrounded by so many children always. It was a reminder of what could have been, and this was not beneficial to my mental health. My depression was getting worse. I would be outside at one of our local barbeques feeling happy one minute then depressed the next. I was in a constant state of flux.

I was taking Xanax every night, and the thoughts of taking my life began to resurface. I never told Robert about this time; he was already working so hard, and I didn't want him to carry the burden of a possibly unhinged maniac. The storm of burdening thoughts and feelings would come and go without warning, and I just dealt with them as they came and went.

I went to see the father at our local church and talked to him again about everything in my life. My escape from reality with the priest seemed like my only haven, besides work and Robert. Even at work, I couldn't escape, but the healing energies of the church always gave me strength. We would talk, for what felt like hours, about all the things I loved, all the pain and depression I had experienced, and life's constant struggles. The priest would always say God only gives us what we can handle, and I replied, "I guess the man thinks I can handle a lot then." I smile to this day, thinking about how much was thrown at me for so many years, knowing God gave me the strength to continue through the most enduring of times. I looked at father and said, "I only ask for two things when I pray; one is for strength to carry on, and the other is for a baby made by love," and he would always smile and say, "one day God will grant you what he believes you need. Have faith, my dear".

Your storm will pass, and you won't remember how you made it through, or even how you managed to survive. You won't even be sure whether the storm was real, but one thing is certain; when you ask me about the five babies I lost, I will never be able to describe or adequately explain the pain and suffering I went through. I can tell you after all that death and loss that I would never be the same person I was. I could have taken my life, but I decided to pick myself up and start living again. That's what being human is all about; we fall only to show we have the chance to be brave and rise from the shadows.

I will never forget how it felt to be pregnant and how I felt when I had five beautiful beings growing in my belly. Every night I would say my prayers and look for the strength to remain positive, and you know what? Life tends to weave itself back together, even through the smallest of frays in its delicate line. I realized that maybe my life was meant to be just the way it was. I guess that's what God had planned for me. Storms come and go, and I had experienced some devilish storms, but I survived. I rise and continue living.

With a newfound sense of living, I continued to work hard, and I was becoming the most exceptional district manager ever to walk this earth. Of course, I say this jokingly. I had the best boss, Pat Kennedy, she would push me hard at work, and I would always respond by breaking over the established threshold. Oh, and obviously, you couldn't forget about my supportive and loving husband. He has always been a beacon of success and hope for my struggling ship at sea. Thank you to all my good friends I had met throughout the years and the beautiful sweet house I lived in. Robert and I could travel whenever we wanted, I thought. We had no kids, no worries, and we were able to take vacations all the time. So, Robert and I ran away into the sunset and lived the rest of our lives, traveling the globe experiencing the wonders of the world. We lived in France, Greece, and Italy, and I even learned to speak three languages! We grew old together and looked back with zero regrets as the sun faded on our little beach of life. Our fairy tale had a worthy ending, I thought. However, after imagining one of the many possible realities that could have unfolded after my epiphany, I knew my existence wasn't set in stone. Life was on course to rotate on itself again. Well, instead of traveling the globe and running off into the sunset with Robert, we decided to go back to where it all started. California, here we come again.

Intermission - What is Normal?

What is normal? Is normal being the average housewife? Is normal going outside every morning and grabbing the same dull paper with nothing but bad news? Is normal just going with the ever-flowing wave of life and wandering meaninglessly in it's current? Well, I was struggling with what my reality had been shaping itself into after all these years of experience. Yes, I was only thirty years old, so my experience could only count for so much. Yet, I remain haunted by the phantoms that had been bestowed upon me since my young adulthood. My struggle of constant fatigue put me off balance, and traveling a lot depressed my emotions even when I was trying my best to stay positive. My phantoms were always around, lurking in the dark, ready to spring on me at any given moment. I didn't have any answers at all, even after all the damn tests I had gone through. This was my normal. I had been living with my phantoms for so long, I guess my genetic makeup was always structured for me to experience these pains. The thing is everyone has something wrong with them. I'm not the only one who struggles with day-to-day phantoms. All the seemingly perfect people, everybody sees in magazines, television, movies, or even your own neighbors simply don't exist. I began to realize that our society is structured on achieving perfection, but who created that idea? Why couldn't I be the model of perfection in my own reality?

What is normal? What is perfection? Is it the person with the highest degree of proficiency, skill, or excellence? Is it a quality trait or feature given to you at birth? I remember reading in a magazine that Beyoncé once sang a song titled "Perfection." Her song highlighted our image of perfection is the disease of a nation. So, maybe none of us are perfect, and we must deal with the reality of being just an average person. Maybe, I am normal; I just carry a little bit of crazy in me. Me and my phantoms.

Chapter 26 - My 6th Pregnancy

Robert and I decided to take another vacation in California. This time, it would be an extended stay. We felt it would be to come back to our roots of love and flourish our garden. Little did I know, not only was our love garden going to thrive, but also a little oasis inside myself. After our return to Ohio, I realized I hadn't had a period in a while. So, I made an appointment with Dr. Wingates, but before that, I went to CVS. I didn't think I was pregnant again, but I thought to myself, "what the hell, one can never except what could happen." So, I peed on the all too familiar stick, and it came back positive. I showed Robert, and we both cried; this time, it was tears of joy. We looked at each other in the eye and said, "whatever happens, we have each other." During our first meeting with Dr. Wingates, he said if I wanted to carry this baby through the first trimester, I needed to take leave from work. After years of working, I finally put my career on hold and focused on the little blossom growing in my belly. Robert wouldn't even let me vacuum the house or lift anything over ten pounds, so I stayed home, and I napped a lot. It was so boring! At fourteen weeks everything looked good, then sixteen weeks came along, and all was good.

I went in for routine blood work every week, and I was gaining weight fast. I was only one hundred & two pounds, but ladies as some of you know pregnancy is a bitch with how much weight you gain. The blood work came back normal, except for a positive marker in gestational diabetes. I had to go on a food plan to control the high blood sugar levels during my pregnancy. Gestational diabetes increases the risk of eclampsia depression, and it also could require a cesarean section. Many times, when a pregnant mother has been diagnosed with gestational diabetes, the baby is still at the time of birth. I prayed to god, please let us get through this.

As time passed, I would hold my growing belly and sit in my rocking chair, talking to the baby all the time. When I was in the nursery, I would sing all the time, so the baby could hear me. My singing voice might be terrible, but

I'm sure my little flower didn't mind. I would play classical music and nursery rhymes through a set of headphones and hold them to my belly, and I would feel tiny kicks. I would giggle and imagine a little baby dancing inside of me. I also started painting large murals in the nursery. I painted Snow White and the seven dwarfs, along with The Lion King, Mickey Mouse, and the Little Mermaid. All the Walt Disney characters I had painted flooded his room with waves of color. Robert wished it was going to be a boy, and I did not care much for the gender, but a little boy would be perfect. We found out a couple weeks later that it was going to be a little boy and Robert was ecstatic. As I was painting in the nursery, I felt compelled to take breaks all the time. I was beginning to feel the numbness in my hands and feet again. I didn't want to stress my little boy inside of me, so I took my time with the murals as a precaution.

I always felt fatigued, but I guess this is normal for pregnant women. Dr. Wingates said I needed to sleep as much as possible after painting or any exercise, so I would sleep. As I laid in bed, the kicks became stronger and stronger, and all the little movements made me feel complete. I would sit in the rocking chair we had custom ordered from California along with the changing table and dresser I also picked out. I even put a bedframe in his room, so when I was tired of painting, I could nap. I started reading as well; that happens when you get pregnant. I remember Robert and I would spend hours in the nursery reading and feeling bliss. Robert and I were planning on going to California again at eighteen weeks. In California, we went shopping at this quaint store called "A Pea in The Pod." It had the cutest pregnancies clothes ever, and of course, I bought as much as I could. Who doesn't look cute with a little baby belly? I did, and my self-confidence was growing alongside my little boy. We had a great trip, and I was feeling pretty good. I was resting a lot, but we managed to do a lot on this trip.

After coming home from that trip, I was tired. My feet were always weak and swollen, and I was so fatigued my vision started going in and out again. I started having nightmares that my baby was going to be stillborn. Fear has an odd way of growing inside someone's mind, and I was worrying. Robert would come home from work, and I would be in the nursery, holding my growing belly, crying because I thought something was going to happen. At twenty weeks Robert had to travel to California again, but Dr. Wingates suggested to no travel anymore. Robert traveled a lot with his job, and I stayed home, getting things ready for our baby. Everything seemed to be going well, and my belly was showing. I was happy.

My girlfriend Becky and Malian were helping me out at home. They would take turns lending me books to read and keeping me company. We would cook food, and I had them on speed dial if anything went wrong. I was folding all the new baby clothing and putting all of them away in the nursery getting ready for the big day. I remember feeling so fatigued after folding baby clothes! I laid down for hours at a time, but I had this strange feeling I had never felt before when I stood up. I felt sharp pains in my belly when I sat down to pee, and I started cramping aggressively. I was in so much pain. All I could do was hold on to the sidewall and whimper in pain. I didn't know what was happening to me. When I wiped myself on the toilet, I discovered blood? I called Malian and told her what was happening, then I called Dr. Wingates. He directed me to go to the ER. Malian and Joe, her husband, came over and took me right away to the ER. I was admitted into the hospital, and they told me I was in labor. This was not good; I was only 20 weeks pregnant.

They called Robert, who was on business in California, to come home as soon as he could. Malian and Joe tried keeping me calm, and Dr. Wingates came into my room to give me medication to stop the labor. I stayed in the hospital for two days under the watch of nurses and Dr. Wingates. Robert got to the hospital and rushed into my room. He spoke to my belly with a comical and worried voice, "Hey, you have to stay in there a little longer my little boy." I smiled at Robert, and he put his face on my belly. As he rested there, he told the baby we loved him; he needed to gestate just a little longer.

From this point on, I was on bed rest until my due date. I could only shower every other day, and it had a timer of three minutes because if I stood longer than that I would start having contractions again. I was also put on perlustrin steroid injections every week in my bottom to help the baby's lungs grow faster just in case they couldn't stop me from going in labor. This scared both Robert and me so much. Every passing week, the doctors administered unique shots and performed ultrasounds. I didn't like the shots, but we loved being able to see our baby growing and moving around in my belly. The little guy really loved kicking me in my bladder all the time. I didn't care though; he was growing, and Robert and I would hold my belly and feel him moving around. I loved it when I would see his little hand or feet up against my skin. This was such an immeasurable joy for both Robert and me. Every day I would read to him and play classical music. He would kick and rummage around inside of me as if he was trying to get his groove on.

Chapter 27 – The 28th Week & Our Beloved First Born

It had been twenty-eight weeks holding a little light inside of me, but my gestational diabetes was getting worse. I was gaining so much weight. Before this pregnancy, I weighed 102 pounds. I had a weigh-in at the hospital, and I was 148 pounds. The ultrasound indicated the baby weighed only five pounds. They put me on a deficient glycemic diet to control my weight gain. When I had visitors, everyone thought we were having twins because I felt like I was 95% composed of a belly.

Week 35 came along, and I was so big and fatigued. I started to notice that I was losing my vision more often, and I had pins and needles all over my body. I told my doctor about my symptoms, and he said my hormones were just going through changes. Week 38 rolled on through, and Dr. Wingates scheduled us to go into the hospital. The time had come. We were so excited and so inexperienced at the same time. They hooked me up to all kinds of wires, and then my water broke. They gave medication to start labor, and I pushed and pushed for what felt like an eternity.

Well, nothing was happening, not even one labor pain. Then they placed a strange teabag in my uterine wall to help move along the process. I didn't have the strength left in me; I had been pushing for so long already. Twenty-one hours had gone by, and the exhaustion was pulling me to sleep. Go figure, the baby we fought for over 8 years of marriage, the pain, fatigue, depression, and five miscarriages later, and he wouldn't come out. What a stubborn little guy; he was definitely my child. He tries to come out months before his time and now doesn't want to come out. Robert was holding my hand, and we both prayed; I pleaded to the man upstairs to help me deliver this baby safely. Then suddenly, I started having contractions.

Dr. Wingates had to perform an epidural on me. He said this would help me with labor because I was too weak to push anymore. All I could see was Robert's face turn completely white. I asked him what was wrong? He shook his head and flinched. The doctor said I just cut you open. Then he told me to push hard. The baby's head began showing. They had to use forceps on the baby's head to pull him out because I couldn't push anymore. Next thing I knew the doctor turned to Robert and asked if he wanted to cut the cord. Robert had a fearful look on his face. I could see the baby, but he wasn't crying. The doctor asked Robert again if he would like to cut the umbilical cord; Robert looked scared, but he grabbed the scissors and tried to cut it, but the scissors slipped. He tried again, but it was a thick cord, and the baby was doused in bodily fluid and blood completely silent. The doctor took the baby's legs and turned him upside down and spanked it. Suddenly, the baby let out a big cry, and voila, we had a baby boy. They handed him to me. I was crying, Robert was crying, and Dr. Wingates even had some tears in his eyes. Our newborn baby had thick black hair and the most handsome face. He weighed six pounds, two ounces, and he was every bit of perfect as I could even imagine. His eyes were closed, but he was crying, and he looked cold. The nurses said we needed to take him to the intensive care unit to check him out. I didn't want to let him go, but doctor Wingates had to stitch me up. The nurse gave me something to relax, and I dozed off into a peaceful sleep.

He was the most beautiful baby; He had thick black hair, ten fingers, ten toes, a terrific smile, and the most piercing eyes like his father. He was perfect. Robert leaned over and kissed me on the head and said, "We have a son." We both cried with so much joy. As the baby was placed into my arms, Robert and I both welcomed him home and said simultaneously said, "We have been waiting for you for years!" Then the nurses took him to the intensive care unit. Robert's brother, Donald, walked with the nurses and stood at the window watching them. At least this is what I was told.

Before I knew it, the nurse came in and handed him to me. My sleep was over quick, but the baby was ready for his first meal. She showed me how to breastfeed him, and he laid there snuggled up against me feeding. We named him, Robert Joseph Deshaies II. His nickname would become, Robby. Breastfeeding him was hard; he was having a hard time with latching on, but the milk was coming, and he had enough. Then the doctor came and told us that our new baby tested positive for jaundice, this is when a yellowish pigmentation of the skin and in the sclera of his eyes occurs. This is caused by bilirubin. They had to keep him in the nursery with a special light on him, so the nurse came and took him after feeding. I quickly fell back to sleep, and my nightmare had finally ended. All the years of pain had seemingly washed away with my first look at Robby. He was a blessing come true and couldn't be more grateful.

Chapter 28 - The Governor & First Weeks

Our brand-new baby boy was the talk of the hospital. All the nurses were talking about him being our miracle baby, and they all loved how handsome he was; He was going to be a lady-killer like his father. Little Robby was swaddled up in my arms, and the nurses asked me if we would be a part of the Governor of Ohio's new campaign for new parents. Robert and I agreed, and our little Robby was already famous. Governor Voinovich came all the way to Findlay, Ohio to talk to us and meet this miracle baby. Robby was three days old when he had his first photoshoot. The Governor and his wife were so sweet, they gave us gifts for Robby.

We even had the local news covering the whole story. After four days in the hospital, we were finally able to take Robby HOME! I was nervous and so happy at the same time. I was also excited to get home and rest because this little guy had put me through so much. One week went by, and Robby had his first check-up. I didn't like the nurses performing the check-up, and neither did Robby. Robert and I cried when they gave him his baby shots. Robby wasn't sleeping much, and he cried all the time; that made me cry. I thought it was my fault. But the doctors said it was because he was a colicky baby. Of course, my little boy had to be as stubborn as me. I laugh today, thinking back. At the time, it was so stressful on me, and of course, I took it as I was doing something wrong. I started to feel depressed again because I felt out of place being a mother.

Postpartum depression is a genuine and scary symptom most women experience post-childbirth. So, on my check-up with Dr. Wingates, I told him I was feeling depressed, and I was having trouble with my memory. I couldn't remember if I had fed Robby or just changed his diapers. "I know that seems crazy," I said to him, but I guess I wasn't crazy at all. This form of depression is caused by the sudden outflux of hormones from giving birth and your body compensating for not having a child to nourish inside oneself anymore. Wingates explained to me the concept of postpartum depression, and this helped put my mind at ease. They gave me a prescription to help me out. It was Xanax... again! I was on the same medication I had been on before when I was having a lot of my phantom attacking me. This must be the medication for everyone in the world, I thought. It seems to be a solution to almost every problem.

Months went by, and I met new moms and became a part of the "mommy" club. We all would go on long walks with Robby in his baby carriage, and I would always have him dressed in the most adorable outfits. He even had the cutest little hats to match. Yes, I was stylistic my whole life, and my newborn wasn't escaping my fashion knowledge. All the moms in the neighborhood would always get together to have coffee and talk about how we felt. There were always talks of each other's babies and the stresses of motherhood; it was a great therapy group now that I look back on it. Robby was growing, and he was so adorable. He started to laugh, and it was a belly laugh that was highly contagious. Robby would sit in his high-chair and play with Cheerios. As he ate them, he would also use his little fingers to flick the Cheerios. As they landed on random surfaces, Robby would burst into laughter; I couldn't help but smile from ear to ear and laugh with him. He loved to play with food, and he was growing into a healthy baby. We went on a vacation to California with him, and I had lost all the weight I had gained during pregnancy! I was back in my post-baby clothing, and I was feeling great. I stopped breastfeeding Robby at five months, so my breasts also returned to normal. On Robby's six-month check-up, the doctors said he was doing great. He was a happy baby boy, and his smile made everyone smile back. I loved every minute I had with him, and Robert would always play with him every minute he could. Robert would toss him around and never fail to catch him. I don't think I had ever seen Robert so gleeful in his life. Finally, we had the family we always wanted. We couldn't have been any happier; life was good.

Chapter 29 – The Question that Sparked Another...

While the Doctors were still checking on Robby during his first weeks, Dr. Wingates asked me if I had a menstrual cycle since giving birth to Robby; I replied no. I thought that was a strange question to ask, so I asked him why? He said I should have had one by now because I stopped breastfeeding Robby at 5 months. Wingates, then, gave me a pregnancy test and had the nurse draw some blood work. Well, after five miscarriages, I guess the pregnant train wasn't stopping any time soon. My pregnancy test came back positive, and I was pregnant again! I couldn't believe it. Robert and I kept it a secret until I was fourteen weeks along, you know when my little belly started to show. Then we started telling everyone we were expecting again! Dr. Wingates said to us at our sixteen-week check-up that everything was going well down under, and the ultrasound looked promising. Robby was going to have a little sister! The current model ultrasound machine the hospital had hooked up was even better than the one they used when I was pregnant with Robby! Robert and I looked at the little monitor and saw our little girls petite head, hands, and feet. Her heartbeat was strong, she was definitely going to be Robert's daughter. Dr. Wingates doubled down, in my opinion, and Robert and I both laughed. I even made a joke back, "that must be why I can't sleep at night, she's always kicking around inside likes she always fighting a match in the ring."

I was feeling extremely fatigued since mid-pregnancy with Robby, and I was about to embark on another strenuous adventure with my baby girl, so I asked the doctor what could help to start sleeping more? He devised that sleeping on my side would provide the most comfort and sleep. Nineteen weeks came along so fast, and my phantoms were striking at my child and me once again; It felt like a home invasion. As a result of my apparitions withering my body down, I had gotten a severe sinus infection that inhibited my breathing. My entire head was in pain from lack of oxygen, and I couldn't eat. I was throwing up everything I ate, and Robert admitted me to the hospital for a week to recover. After coming home, absolutely drained of energy, I had to focus on taking care of myself if I was going to bring another healthy baby to term. It was so hard to take care of myself, let alone take care of Robby. He was still just an infant, barely a toddler, but nothing was going to stop me from caring for my child. It would be cruel if I had to choose, but that was never an option for me. I fought so hard to have my little boy; he was my everything. He and Robert were my world & my family; nothing was going to take them away.

On top of my sinus infection, stopping me from being at my best, my little Robby was fighting a bad cold as well. His little smile had fractured into this heartbroken look on his face that absolutely killed me when we made contact. I couldn't bear to look at my child in such pain. When I took him into the doctor's office, they said he needed to be hospitalized. He had a human respiratory syncytial virus, and He was admitted to the hospital for a week. I slept at the hospital, every night, with Robby. I wasn't going to leave him. As I watched our little boy, rest in his small hospital carriage, I regularly dozed off from the sheer exhaustion. Robert would come to the hospital and see us in between work; this helped take most of the load of parenthood off. Robert is such an amazing dad. Every minute he could hold or play with Robby, he was there. It appeared as if Robert was a magician, I would glance away for a second and "presto!" he was standing in the doorway. No, he didn't have a rabbit in his hat.

After being in the hospital for a week, Robby was finally recovering, and they let him go home. He was looking alive, and he started to play with his trains and watch "Snow White and the Seven Dwarfs" by Walt Disney, once again. Snow White was his favorite movie, I think. We played it at least twelve times a day, while Robby would march around the house and sing all the lyrics to "High Ho" while holding his little hammer. It was quite a spectacle.

One day, Robert came home with an old computer laptop and started to show Robby how to work it. I couldn't believe my eyes; Robby was really learning how to read and operate a computer. He was so smart for such a little baby boy; I think I might have given birth to a genius. Robby was turning one year old, and we had the biggest celebration ever. I know he really wasn't aware of what was going on, but this was a real celebration. He was our miracle baby, and I was blessed enough to be pregnant again with my little girl on her way. My belly was so big it looked like ¾ of a bowling ball hanging from my stomach. Robert was so sweet as well, to go along with what felt like my body morphing into this adorable, round, fluff ball again, He gained weight with me. He began eating all his cravings along with all my funky cravings. It was quite hysterical when Robby would play with Robert's chubby cheeks. It made me laugh quite a bit.

This pregnancy was going so well. My check-ups were signaling, "all good," and I thought if I kept myself busy with Robby time would fly by, and my due date would be coming fast. As I rested in either my chair or on the floor of our house, Robby would play endlessly. He was an energizer bunny with no outage of power. I would teach him how to talk and walk, and I started painting again when Robby would nap. I began to paint the new nursery for our little girl at every chance I could. I painted a large tree with Bambi, Thumper, and Flower from the movie "Bambi" by David Hand. I also painted big fluffy clouds and adorable angels flying overhead. Her nursery was decorated with custom furniture from California, and it glistened with all white wicker. Dabs of soft pink and greens highlighted her bedding; it was my little girl's haven. Robby would sit with me as I painted, and he would always reach and hold my belly. Every time he grabbed on, he would say, "b-b-ba-by." I couldn't help but giggle. While I was still pregnant with our daughter, my friends kept asking me to paint their nurseries. This made me happy, and with the doctor's approval, I took up their many offers. Wingates said if I kept eating well and making sure I rested in-between, everything would be alright.

Robby and I would go to our neighbor's house, and he would play as I painted other nursery's for clients. It appeared that my phantom pains were not so bad during this time. My hand or foot would go numb occasionally, but I just thought it was from being pregnant again. My hands were tired from long days of painting and carrying all this extra weight. Art had always been my love, and I adored bringing walls to life, knowing that other babies were coming home to such colorful and lively nurseries. This made me so happy, but also very fatigued.

I was thirty weeks pregnant with our little girl, and time had flown by. I couldn't believe how easy it was; I only gained 28 pounds. I was done with all my commissioned murals and thought, "why not paint our new deck off the back of the house?"

It was the month of May, and summer was approaching. Robby was walking full-time now; he never even crawled. He would sit on his little butt with one leg behind him like a monkey. He was fully walking at nine months old. The summer heat was wonderful as I worked on painting the deck. I was very active during this pregnancy. Robert would come home and play for hours with our little guy, so I could rest. Robert's brother, Donald, would come over and watch Robby so we could have a date night. They loved eating chocolate chip ice-cream together and watching old films. Robby was growing smarter with each film he watched. It was quite amazing to see our little boy gain so much in such a short amount of time. Donald still talks about those days with both Robby and me to this day. I thought, "wow" I have it all. I have a loving husband, a beautiful, healthy, and happy baby boy, and a little girl on her way. The phantom pains weren't so bad anymore. Only the pins and needles in my hands and feet. Occasionally, my left eye would go blurry on me, but nothing was going to stop me from enjoying those early years of motherhood. This was my normal, and I was okay with it.

Chapter 30 – Robby's Early Life & His Little Sister's Birth

It was a scorching summer day in June, so I decided not to paint the deck that afternoon. Robby and I went to the Findlay mall instead. He loved going to see all the new trains at the toy store. We had gotten him a big train table with all kinds of track and train configurations; it was called "Thomas the Tank Engine," and every toy train had its own name. Robby would play for hours mixing and matching dozens of different tracks and would love to see the trains just go around and around. I would buy him a new one every week; he was quite a spoiled little one, but hey, he was my little guy. We would play for hours together with his trains, and we would voice ourselves over each character to have a conversation with each other.

Robby was a fast learner; he was barely one year old, and he already learned how to read. He had a great imagination and was always tinkering with his hands. Robby would look at his giant train table and ponder what he could do next, he was like Rodin's thinking man. I would look at him playing with his trains, and he would make me giggle with every hand motion and word originating from his chubby cheeks. As we would sit there, Robby would come up to me and tell me stories that he came up with on the fly. I couldn't believe how fast he was growing. As I looked down on my little boy, I remembered how hard it was on me carrying him to term. It was so worth every minute of tears, worrying, and pain I went through to call this child my own. He was our miracle baby. That night after our day at the mall, I put Robby down for a nap. I laid down as well, but I was feeling super fatigued and tired. I couldn't sleep, so I thought I was going to go outside to finish painting the deck. I just wanted it ready, so when our baby girl came, everything would be down.

It was four o'clock, and the sun was on the other side of our house, so the temperature was cool outside. I remember placing the last stroke of paint on the deck and thinking to myself how proud I was to finish such a task. As I was cleaning up the paint supplies, I started to cramp; I was thirty-three weeks into the pregnancy. I went into the house and called the doctor's office. I told them about the cramping, and they told me to monitor myself in intervals. It felt like I was in labor; the cramps came every ten minutes. They told me to lay down, put my feet up, and drink lots of water. Robert came home, and I told him what was going on. It was weird, but this pregnancy was going well, so I just laid down and relaxed while listening to music. I remember Robby waking up and walking into my bedroom with me and said, "M-mom-my is b-baby coming?" I said, "no, honey, not for four more weeks,"; he giggled. We had everything ready, just in case.

My bag was even packed and prepared for the hospital. Our sweet, little, baby girl's clothing was hanging up in her closet waiting for her. We also ordered a new Stoller that could hold two. The basinet was all ready and next to Robert and I's bed as well. Robby said, "Mom-my can I get gi-ft from ba-by room?", I said, "yes." He came back into my room with an outfit and diapers and said, "bab-y need this!", it was an outfit and diapers; he was so smart and loving! It was time for Robby's bath, and I remember kneeling next to the tub. I started cramping again; now, I was becoming worried.

I called Robert, and he took over the bath while I went to bed, feeling ill.

It was three in the morning, and I got up to pee. I was cramping even worse than before, so I started to monitor my cramps again. The contractions were 6 minutes apart. When I wiped myself, I found spotting and bleeding all over the tissue. We called Dr. Wingates, and he ordered us to get to the hospital. Robert and I were so scared. I was turning thirty-four weeks that day, and it was way too soon for our little girl to be born. We arrived at the hospital around 4:30 AM. By the time the doctor came into the room, I was in full labor; there was no stopping it.

My water broke, and I began to worry even more. The nurses tried to give me an epidural, but it only blocked the pain on my right side. I could feel EVERYTHING on my left side of my body! Giving birth is no easy task, whew. Before we knew it, they had me ready to give birth. They said the baby was in distress and her heartbeat was lowering; this worried the doctors, nurses, and scared the living hell out of Robert and me. I pushed for about 30 minutes, and she finally came out. Her umbilical cord was wrapped around her neck, and she was barely clinging to a single breath. Robert looked terrified; she was so small and completely blue. I started to cry. The nurses rushed her straight to the infant intensive care unit. Robert held my hand, kissed me on my forehead, and we both prayed.

The nurses were so kind and comforting to us. Thirty minutes passed, and they came back into the room with our baby girl; we named her Simone, after Robert's grandmother. I told you I loved that name from the first time I heard it. She was a petite four pounds, three ounces. Robert was able to hold her in the palm of his hand, that's how small she was.

They told me to try to breastfeed her. She immediately latched on to me and started breastfeeding. The nurse was so shocked. All the nurses called her, "the little boxer." As I looked at my little Simone, I remembered when I met Simone Rivest for the first time. I remember

Robert's grandmother walking down her stairwell like an old black-and-white film looking like a Hollywood starlet. She was so put together and so beautiful. Everything she did was with elegance and grace; I remember watching her make these little candies, from her own recipe, while she had on a white apron with a beautiful dress under it. Her hair was pulled back, and she was so full of life and looked at me with the most gracious smile. She was so beautiful, and she was the Matriarch of the family. I remember saying to Robert that day if we ever had a little girl, I wanted to name her Simone. As I snapped out of my flashback, I looked down and gazed at Robert and I's new daughter, her eyes lit up the room like an angel visiting. She was going to become even more graceful and elegant than Simone Rivest, I thought.

Unfortunately, Robert's grandmother passed away before we had children. Simone Rivest's spirit lives on in our little girl, and I couldn't be prouder.

She was a fighter; strong and beautiful just like Robert's Grandmother. She was so happy but so little. We stayed in the hospital for a week, and she gained two pounds.

They said we could go home, finally. I remember Robby and Robert walking into the hospital room, and I gave Robert Simone; he kissed her so softly. Robby was fifteen months old, and he came over to Robert to see his little sister. It was the most precious moment ever as he gave her a kiss on her forehead. I will always remember that forever. As my husband held our daughter, I looked at him and realized he stood by me every step of the way; through thick and thin he never gave up hope, even when I was at my worst. Robert was holding our baby girl and right next to him was our miracle boy who was now fifteen months old walking and talking. This moment in time, I have imprinted in my mind, and I look back on it often; even to this day. It was time to go home from the hospital with our baby girl Simone. When we arrived home, we all sat on the couch together. Robby looked at both of us and said, "I love her Mommy and Daddy," Robert and I couldn't help but well up with tears of joy. Robby was into trains at the time, and he went to grab his favorite train, Thomas the train, and he handed it to his little sister. She couldn't fully grab onto any objects yet, and he looked confused. I smiled and said she doesn't know how to hold things yet, but soon you will be playing together; Robby giggled. I loved Robby's giggles, they were so contagious; they made everyone happy and laugh with so much joy.

Our first week home was a little crazy. Robby was still in diapers, and I now had a newborn baby girl to take care of as well. Trying to feed them both at the same time wasn't easy. I was breastfeeding Simone every two hours, then playing with Robby, then trying to clean the house, and trying to keep myself organized. About three weeks after being home, I was feeling overwhelmed and very fatigued. I wasn't sleeping, and Robby still would only sleep for two hours at a time. In between Simone's breastfeeding, Robert would be with Robby giving him a bottle of formula. Talk about sleep deprived! That was Robert and I's life now. You could take a picture of us and put it up on a billboard and advertise this is as parenthood. Running on zero sleep, with a ponytail, no makeup, and no time for myself; yup, that explains early parenthood very well. Simone had gotten all her baby shots a little while after being home, and she was doing so well. My phantom symptoms, however, weren't going so well. My vision problems resurfaced, and there were days I didn't even have time to shower, let alone have time to look good. I was able to go back to the gym again after back-to-back pregnancies; thank god for gym daycare. It was a blessing that I could work out, and the lovely girls working the daycare took such good care of my two babies. I was feeling fatigued all over, and I thought it was from training at the gym and the exhaustion from taking care of my children. I started to lose the baby weight again.

We hired a part-time babysitter, Tristin, to help play with Robby and Simone, so I could have "me" time. Even with Tristin's fantastic help, I still felt overwhelmed. I was sleep-deprived and continuously fatigued. I went to my doctor, and they ran some blood work because I felt concerned. It all came back normal, and the doctor said I was young and healthy, again! I told him about all the phantom symptoms I had been observing over the years and told him they were getting worse. I felt like no one believed me. He said that all new mothers go through this, and once again he gave me a prescription for Xanax. I swear every doctor made me feel like I was simply crazy. I remember one day when I was at the park with Robby and Simone; Robby was running around, and Simone was in the baby swing. I was pushing her, and she felt like a thousand pounds when she was only three months old. Holding her was like holding the biggest baby in the world! My hands always stung with pins and needles while my legs felt like overcooked noodles. I was always feeling weak, and my legs would go limp on me. I was training at the gym four days a week, and I had lost all the baby weight. I was now back to my normal weight of one hundred and two pounds. I trained my body hard to get back in shape, and I looked healthy and good on the outside. Inside, however, felt so weak. Every day when Robert would get home, I would rest, and he would take care of the children and play. Don't get me wrong I had it all; the perfect life, a handsome, loving husband, two beautiful babies, and a beautiful home were all ours, but the pain was overwhelming at some points. We can't always be at our 100% strength all the time. I kept taking the Xanax and doing everything I could to look and feel normal, but nothing was providing me with a solution. I was a great mom; just ask my children now. I played with them, I loved them, I set up play dates with all the other moms, and we did what moms do together. We watched all the kids play while we talked over coffee. It's the simple things sometimes that I think we all occasionally overlook that provides so much pure pleasure.

Chapter 31 – March 2000

Before I knew it, Robby was now two years old, and Simone was crawling everywhere. We would go for walks down by the river to feed the ducks, take trips to the mall, and go to the country club. They would play with other children at the pool with their little floaties on. Robert's career was taking off, and he was moving up the corporate ladder fast. This meant he was traveling a lot more, so Tristin was helping me more than before. She was working 20 hours a week for us alone. I was able to get my nails done and have time with other moms for lunch dates, so I could rest and recuperate. I remember telling my friend Cara about all the phantoms I was experiencing, and she also said I was just fatigued. My friend Cecelia, who was always so sweet, also had a baby girl named Caroline; she and Robby were almost the same age, so we were always together while the kids played. We would talk about how I was upset and frustrated by my doctors all the time. Why couldn't we come up with a solution for fatigue for mothers yet? Caffeine can only do so many ladies. I was so irritated with doctors telling me the same damn thing for years. I knew deep down, there was something wrong with me; I just didn't know what.

Time passed, I kept my phantom pains to myself and carried on with my life. I got up every day, placed my makeup on, and did what every other mom out there did; our job. Our job has a simple premise, be a good mother and a good wife. Simple instructions, right? Well, it's a lot harder than those clauses. Before we knew it, Simone was walking, and she and Robby were inseparable. They played so well together. We also were having Simone baptized the same weekend. Our house was full of family; Robert's mother Judith flew out from Massachusetts, and Robert's father Donald also flew out for the baptism. It was also Simone's first birthday. We were having a massive celebration. After the big party, I started packing for our family trip to Walt Disney World, Florida. We flew out on Simone's birthday, June 19th. We checked into the hotel, and the kids were so tired, so were we. We did everything we could the next day. We saw every attraction Disney had to offer, I think Robert and I both turned back time because we were having a blast with our children. The laughter and playing made for a fantastic trip. There was one day on our vacation we went to the wild animal park. We had the double stroller and were ready for a long day of fun. Robby was so into dinosaurs, and Simone really wanted to see all the Walt Disney princesses. We had been at the park for about three hours, and it started to rain. What a bummer! That didn't stop our fun, though. We stayed and kept walking around the park, then suddenly the rain shifted into hurricane-like winds, and the rain was hitting us from all different directions. The kids were crying because this rain felt like rocks. Robert had Robby, and I had Simone; we were trying to get on the tram to get to our rental car. Poor Robby and Simone were so scared. We finally got to the car. It looked like we were doused by a fire hydrant worth of water. As we were driving back to our hotel, Robby suddenly said, "Daddy, do you think the clouds are mad?" Robert and I both looked and shook our heads, yes. Then Simone and Robby said, "please don't make the clouds mad again." The very next day we stayed at the hotel and went swimming with the kids; we had so much fun. Simone was such a cute, and adorable baby girl with curly brown hair and Robby was starting to lose all his baby fat. We all got tans, and Simone's tan lines were so dam adorable because of her rolls. When she moved her arms in-between her rolls, her tan exposed white lines. This was such an incredible trip with our two children. We were gone for ten days, and it was so much fun. I think Robert and I had just as much fun as the kids.

After arriving home from Florida, we were back in our regular routine, and the kids were sleeping well. I was tired of traveling, and I took up my motherly duties again. Robert went back to work and traveling again. Four weeks later I really wasn't feeling well. I thought that I must have gotten sick from traveling. I put the kids down for naps, and I would typically do housework, but that day I really wasn't feeling well. Everything was going crazy pins, and needles streaked across my body, and I felt so weak. It took all I had just to keep track of time; I didn't even get dinner ready that night. I lied down and fell asleep. As I woke up, Robert was home; I didn't even hear him come into the house. He had Robby and Simone, and they were playing in the playroom. All I could hear was laughter. As I walked in, Robert, Robby, and Simone were dancing and singing. They all looked at me and said, "Mommy you don't look very good," and suddenly I ran to the bathroom; I threw up over and over, and I thought I had the flu.

Robert looked at me and asked when my last period was? Then I realized I had not had a period ever since Simone was born. I was still breastfeeding her, and she was only thirteen months old. How could I be pregnant? I was still breastfeeding Simone and had barely been a year since her birth. We went to CVS, and I bought three pregnancies tests. Everyone indicated I was pregnant. We both thought, "wow," another baby. So, we made an appointment with good old Dr. Wingates, and he gave me another pregnancy test; they performed some blood work and gave me an ultrasound exam. I was six weeks pregnant. We were all in the room, and Robby asked,

"Daddy what is that?", Robert replied, "you and Simone are going to have another brother or sister." Simone had the cutest little grin, and Robby giggled with laughter. I looked at Dr. Wingates and said, "I can't believe it!"; Robert and I got pregnant on Simone's 1st birthday. I even asked Robert to wait until Simone was 1 year old before we tried again for another baby. Well, we didn't even try, and it happened. God had blessed us on her first birthday. Robert and I were ecstatic we couldn't believe it. After eight years of trying to have a baby, we couldn't stop getting pregnant. Please don't get me wrong, I was the happiest mother ever. I felt so blessed, and Robert was beaming with excitement. This meant this baby's due date was going to be March 20th; the same birth month Robby and I shared.

We got home, and I needed to take a nap. I was emotionally and physically tired. I began to think, and I was worried about how this pregnancy would be. Robby was such a hard pregnancy on me, and Simone was born pre-mature at thirty-four weeks. We went to Dr. Wingate's office a little later that week, and he confirmed I was 6 weeks along. It hit me right then and there that we were expecting another baby! The first trimester was hard; I was fighting constant exhaustion and wasn't sleeping well. My dreams were consistent nightmares, and every night, I felt like I was trying to run and scream, but something was holding me back. I also had the same dreams when I was pregnant with Robby and Simone.

I guess it's something moms go through; the fear of the unknown. I pondered, "Is the baby going to be ok?", well I prepared myself mentally for anything to happen. I carry this baby all the way through until it's time for him or her to come, I thought to myself. I did everything to keep this pregnancy healthy. I took all my vitamins and slept when Robby and Simone slept. I rested when I could, but I still had to be a mom, wife, friend, and keep myself mentally together. I went into the hair salon and had them cut all my long hair; it was time for something a little different. Picture as a Chanel model in the 50's with "The New Look." It was short and cute, and I felt glamorous. When Robert got home, he was so surprised that I cut my long hair. I said I needed a change and I wanted to watch my hair grow back! Robert loved my hair long, but he was going to wait for it to grow back. We were still living in our home in Findlay, Ohio. Our neighborhood was great. We all had kids, and they all played together. The parents of each household got along very well, and it was a perfect fit.

Having a community around us was very comforting to me. We even bought a minivan, just like all the moms.

Chapter 32 – Baby for Christmas?

Most of the time, I kept myself preoccupied with taking care of my newborn babies, but occasionally, I needed to escape and observe some sequestered moments for myself. What better way to spend my time than to work at some philanthropies, I thought? I started to volunteer for the American Cancer Society to pass a lot of my time. I would build Christmas trees with all the other volunteers during their annual charity event. I had been a volunteer for the society for three years, and the first tree I ever decorated was a tree I named, "Toys in the Attic." This tree was riddled with old fashion toys made from an amalgamation of metals and wood just like the early days; it was perfect for a little boy. Our first Christmas with Robby, we bought the tree I designed for Robby at the night of the auction. The following year I decorated a tree called "Winter Wonderland." It was filled with snowmen, hot cocoa-cups, snowflakes, and blue ribbon. We knew we were having a little girl that year, so we bought that tree for our little girl. Christmas is Robert's all-time favorite holiday. During the Christmas season, our family home was always glistening with Christmas cheer. Our house was so adorable. We decorated everything; Robert wanted no less than everything covered in Christmas delight. We had our family tree filled with Lennox ornaments, Robby's tree full of toys from the attic, and Simone's tree shined with winter wonder.

After most of the decorating had been completed, I had another ultrasound checkup for the expecting baby. Robert came home from work, and we all went to the doctors together. Dr. Wingates was so cute when we arrived. He asked the kids what they wanted for Christmas, and Robby replied with toys and a baby brother; he even added a "please" at the end. Simone said she wanted princesses and a baby sister, also remembering her manners. We all giggled. The kids got to see the baby moving around in my belly, and Robby pointed to the umbilical cord and inquired what, as he put it, "that weird string thing" was. I replied, "that's how Mommy feeds the baby," Robby and Simone had the funniest faces and said, "but you feed us at the kitchen table?"; We all laughed. A moment in time to remember. The checkup was great, and I weighed in at one-hundred and twenty-four pounds; my belly had returned to its fluff-ball features. The funny thing was, if someone was looking at me from behind, they couldn't even tell if I was pregnant. Robby and Simone would talk about Santa Clause almost every day in anticipation of the big celebration on Christmas Day. They would ask if the new baby was coming when Santa came? Our friends across the street were expecting on Christmas Day, and to Robby and Simone, they thought their sibling was going to be born that day as well.

I was now six months pregnant with our baby boy. This pregnancy was going well, but I was just fatigued and always tired. Somedays I couldn't even remember if I had fed Robby and Simone. I would forget laundry in the wash for days and then remember. I loathed having to rewash everything again. My left eye was always blurry, and my hands were still dropping the most random objects. I remember trying to pick up Simone from her crib, and my hand let go; this really scared me. I started to cry, and it scared me to think I had almost dropped my little girl. Thank god she was still over the crib. My belly was growing more significant, and the baby was growing as well; he kicked a lot. Simone and Robby would love holding my stomach to feel their little brother move around. Simone was struggling to keep healthy shortly after her first birthday and was diagnosed with RSV, the same affliction Robby had when he was a little guy. She was admitted to the hospital and recovered there. Shortly after that scare, she would consistently fight with colds, so I was stressed out all the time trying to do everything I could to keep her healthy.

I remember talking to my mother about Simone, and she suggested taking all her stuffed toys from her room, just like my mother did when I was always sick as a young child. I did, and we went to the doctor's office. Simone was always having trouble breathing, so she went through asthmatic treatments to keep her lungs open. Robert and I took turns rocking her to sleep as we gave her the breathing treatments with Prednisone and Albuterol. Simone always had to have her stuffed toy

Barney by her side when she slept. Simone would hold and drag him around all the time, no matter where she went. I don't think I can recall a single moment during Simone's childhood where she let that purple dinosaur go.

We had to buy another one, so when she was sleeping, we could wash the dirty one. Robert and I knew every song that Barney would sing so we could sing along with Simone. She really didn't like the asthma treatments, but it was the only thing keeping her lungs working at the time. Due to her premature birth, Simone was more susceptible to bronchoconstriction and Chronic Obstructive Pulmonary Disease. We asked the doctors what would be best for her health, and they advised we move to a more medial climate. Robert and I knew just the place where Simone would grow up healthy. Robby was two and a half, and Simone was fourteen months old when Robert and I began to look for our new home in California.

Chapter 33 - Looking for a Home & The New Baby Boy

Robert, the kids, and I all took a trip to California to begin our search for the new family house. Robert and I met an excellent realtor by the name of Jeff Jagger. He was incredibly supportive, sweet, and very kind. While we were out there looking for homes, we also had such a great vacation and took the kids to Disneyland California. I think we walked the whole park that day. Simone didn't have any asthma attacks or breathing issues in a short time in California, and this pushed us even more to find the perfect house. We went to the beach and walked outside all the time. The weather was always warm and sunny; we all loved it here.

We arrived back home in Ohio, and immediately, Simone started getting sick again. It was a consistent schedule admitting and readmitting to the hospital. She struggled with RSV and Asthma still, and we knew we had to move back to California. I didn't have a problem with when Robert and I lived there when we first got married, and we loved it. Robby and Simone were both conceived in California. I thought this must have symbolized a good luck charm for us. Our retailer, Jeff Jagger, was becoming a good friend to us and he continued to look for homes for us while we were in Ohio. Jeff was amazing, and his wife, Michelle, and two girls, Emily and Lauren lived in Mission Viejo. Emily and Lauren were around the same ages as Robby and Simone, so that was perfect for playdates. We wanted a four-bedroom home, and to be honest, I was sticker shocked at how much the prices had gone up. My Best Friend, Jenna lived, in California, and I wanted to live somewhere in between them and the freeway. I know highways are ugly, but it would be easier for Robert since he would be traveling a lot more. We found three homes we loved, but the realtors took other offers, and we still hadn't sold our house back in Ohio yet.

This was stressful on Robert and I. Simone was always on breathing treatments when we were in Ohio, but the whole time we were in California, she was fine; just like the doctors had pointed out. Wow, I actually agreed with them for once. I figured if Simone was doing so well in California, then maybe all my phantom symptoms would go away as well. We were in Ohio and started preparing to sell the house; we packed up as much as we could. At this time, we had gone through three storage spaces inside our home. The house in Ohio was over five-thousand square feet with four bedrooms, an office, a family room, a living room, a playroom, a kitchen, and the dining room. I was so used to living in such a big house. We wanted to find a house about the same size in California, so Jeff had a big job trying to find us a home. I was stressing about Simone's health and just wanted our house to sell and move to California.

I was running around with Robby and Simone at thirty-three weeks pregnant when Robert flew out to California to look at some homes. I stayed in Findlay because I was too close to term. No sooner had Robert came home, and before we knew it, I was turning thirty-five weeks pregnant, and I was going into labor. We went straight to the hospital, and the nurse said I was only dilating two centimeters and they were going to send me home. The contractions kept coming, and I told her I knew that the baby was coming; she kept saying, "no"! This upset me, and I demanded, "I'm not leaving until Dr. Wingates shows up." My contractions were now five minutes apart and that damn nurse kept telling me that they were going to send me home. I told Robert I wasn't leaving because I was in so much pain. I couldn't even feel my feet! I was becoming even more frustrated, and I broke out crying because this damn nurse wasn't even listening to me. The monitors indicating my contractions were going crazy, and I was now two minutes apart. I remember saying to Robert that it hurt so bad. I was hysterically crying when Dr. Wingates walked in to check on me when my water broke. I was dilated at six centimeters now in full labor. They wouldn't administer an Epidural, so I had to go through labor with no pain medication.

Robert simply rubbed my head and kissed me. Robby and Simone were home with Robert's brother, Donald, sleeping. We left the house in the middle of the night and didn't want to disturb our little angels. After six hours of excruciating labor, our baby boy was born at thirty-five weeks on February 20th, 2001. They let me kiss him and then took him straight to ICU. After he was born, Robert followed them to the ICU unit with our baby boy. I was so tired and drained when they gave me something to take the edge off. I told Doctor Wingates I wanted to have my tubes tied. I didn't even discuss with Robert, because I was partly delusional. I couldn't imagine having another baby after the third time, so I signed the papers, and before I knew it, I was asleep. Robert arrived in the room with our new baby boy shortly after a quick rest. He was so little and very yellow, but he was hungry, so I started to breastfeed him. He was like Simone and started breastfeeding naturally. As soon as our little boy was finished, the doctor and nurses came into the room and said they were ready for surgery.

Robert looked shocked and asked the doctor, "What surgery?" I told him I was getting my tubes tied and he was so upset. Dr. Wingates came to my rescue, and said, "Robert her body can't take another pregnancy. She has had five miscarriages and three difficult childbirths. It's time to tie up the tubes. Besides, you have three beautiful children, and God has blessed you, sir". I looked at Robert, and I said, "I love you" because let's be honest, I was going to have this surgery whether Robert liked it or not. Off I went to get my tubes tired as Robert held our new baby boy in his hands sleeping. I was being prepped for surgery when Dr. Wingates came over to me and asked if I was ready, I said "yes." Before I knew it, they were walking me up to surgery, and a warm daze fell over me. As I woke up, Robert was there waiting for me, and the baby was hungry again, so I nursed him for the second time. As I held our sweet baby boy, we discussed baby names. Robert wanted him to have his middle name, but I said we already have a son named after you. I wanted to call him Grant or Ethan, but Robert won. We named him Joseph Christopher Deshaies. All three of our children were named after Robert's side of the family.

The doctor came into the room and said our baby had a bad case of Jaundice, like Robby. Joseph was incubated in a carriage with a circular ring shining with a special light to heal the pigmentation for about twenty-four hours. I nicknamed him my little glowworm. Robert went home to take care of Robby and Simone while I stayed in the hospital with Joseph. I remember Robert walking in to see me along with the kids. They were so damn cute, and I missed them so much. Robby asked, "what is that mommy?" I laughed and said, "this is your little brother, Joseph. He's a glowworm". Robby's eyes opened so wide and said, "WHAT! He's a toy?", we all laughed so hard. Simone asked, "c-c-can I kiss h-him mommy, or will his light go out if I k-k-kiss him?", we laughed again. I told both them they could kiss him, and I also reassured them he wouldn't stop glowing. Robby, Simone, and I kept calling Joseph our little glowworm. We had a perfect family. Two boys and one girl that Daddy could spoil all the time. Before we knew it, we were heading to our house back in Findlay. Everyone came over to see our newborn baby with his yellow light. All my friends and family called him the cutest little glowworm. Joseph was gaining weight, and after two weeks of being my little glowworm, he no longer gleamed yellow. We didn't need the light any longer, but he will always be my little glowworm.

Joseph was always hungry, and this time breastfeeding was different. Joseph would finish all the milk in one breast, so I would have to pump the other breast. Our freezer had so much milk we didn't have room for more. He didn't like the bottle. At my checkup, I told Dr. Wingates about all the milk I had stored, and he said I could bring it into his office every week for another little baby boy. This little boy's mother couldn't breastfeed, and the baby was allergic to all the formula, so my milk helped raise another beautiful baby. I thought that was so cool! Not only was I able to breastfeed my own baby, but I was now breast feeding another baby. Every week we would bring a large frozen case of breast milk to the doctor's office to help any other child who needed my excess supply of nutrition. Life seemed to be moving fast, and my phantom pains were not that bad after Joseph was born. I thought to myself, "maybe this time they will go away for good." I was happy we were moving to California, a new light shined on the horizon, and my family and I were ready for it.

Chapter 34 – Thankful, An Interlude

Before we moved, Joseph was baptized, and Jenna even flew out because we ordained her as his godmother. Joseph was now 3 months old, and everyone came into town for the baptism. Jenna just had her son, Wesley who was only six months old, but she still made it out. Robert's mother and father also flew out for the baptism, and we had a big party to celebrate. I stood at the altar with Robert and his brother, Donald; the godfather to all our children. Jenna stood next to me while Joseph was baptized. Robby, Simone, and Joseph were all born in the same Hospital, brought home to the same warm house, and baptized in the same church. How awesome is that? I felt so blessed that day. Robert held Joseph as I kneed in front of the altar and spoke silently. I bowed my head and thanked God for all the blessings he sent Robert and me, and I promised him that I would be the best mother to my children as best I could. I will always thank God for my husband, family, and friends. His blessings have ever come at the right time. I also asked him to please help me with all my phantom pains, and I even asked God that when I arrived in heaven one day to please allow me to see our five other children, I miscarried. Until then, I promised I would always do my best to help others and care for my family and friends the best way I could. I would continue to do charitable works in his name. Every day I did the best I could to keep everything together, and when I would see the faces of our children, I would look up and say thank you to God for blessing us with this beautiful family.

Chapter 35 - The Big Move

Robert, I, and all three kids went out to California to keep looking for a new home. We stayed at The Colony in Newport Beach and lived there until we found a new home. Simone was looking healthy as ever, and Robby and Joseph were too. I loved it! We were close to Fashion Island and the kids, and I would spend hours walking. I had two in the stroller and Joseph in a Baby Bjorn. People would look at me puzzled and ask how old they all were, and I would tell them three years old, two years old, and 6 months. I always got the same response, "Wow, I guess you got it all done fast," I would laugh and smile and say God blessed us. I was so happy, and the phantoms appeared to have disappeared. Robert had discovered a new development being constructed in Dana Point. It was this cute little beach town twenty-five minutes down the coast. We went to look, and we loved it. The development had fifteen new homes behind a gated community, and it was very close to a church, preschool, and elementary. Everything seemed to be falling into place, but the house wouldn't be ready for four more months.

We traveled back to Ohio to get everything finished for sale. We sold the house to a doctor who was starting a family of his own. His wife loved all the murals I had painted, and they thought it was the perfect fit. After three weeks, we had everything packed up and journeyed back to California. This time we lived at the DoubleTree Hotel until our new home was finished. We had two rooms with a conjoined door in the middle, so we could see the kids. This was very stressful living in a two-room suite. We would go to the house every other day to check on the progress; we hoped to move in sooner.

I was so happy to have Jenna close to me, and Wesley, her infant son, was so adorable. I loved being able to see them all the time. We planned playdates all the time because our backyard was ready. All the kids would play together in the warm California sun, and everything looked right in the world. We discovered all the parks all around southern California and went to every single one of them. Jenna, I, and the kids were always together, and coffee was flowing all the time. We talked about our lives, and I remembered how much I loved this woman. She was my best friend then and remains so today. She is the sister I never had.

Robert and I were so excited to move into our brand-new home; it was a four thousand square feet house, with five bedrooms, and three baths. Our back and front yard was all dirt still, so that would be our very first task moving in.

It took me two weeks to unpack and put everything away. Joseph wasn't even walking yet, so he had the bedroom downstairs while Simone and Robby slept upstairs. Simone never liked her room up there even when I painted it for her. Robby's room had all his toys and books and was already showing signs of messiness. Joseph was still in a crib because he was only six months old. He was learning to crawl, and with his sibling's help, we were up in no time. The kids kept me busy for sure. I weighed about 105 pounds, and I was always on the run. The fatigue was beginning to build up. When the kids were bathed and put to bed, I would go to lay down and rest.

Robert was working for Microsoft at the time and traveling a lot. Jenna was my companion when Robert was gone. She was so close to us this that it made things much easier on me. She would teach me all the roads and highlighted all the essential places to go since my last time in California. Of course, the malls were number one on that list. California freeways were crazy, the speed limits were so much higher than Ohio. I joined a 24-Hour Fitness and went there two days a week. They had daycare, so that was a nice break for me. Robert also got all of us season passes to Disneyland.

I would take the kids there when Robert would leave to go to work in Seattle, Washington, for the week. I would make plans to keep the kids busy because our backyard wasn't finished. I would pack up the baby backpack with everything anyone would ever need. The double-seated stroller for Robby and Simone was also packed, and the Baby Bjorn was strapped on the front of me. Joseph would sit in it like a baby kangaroo, and we would spend all day and night at Disneyland. The kids loved it, and I did too. When Joseph needed to nap, Robby would walk next to me, and I would put Joseph down in the carriage to sleep. I would watch Robby and Simone go on all the rides, and they liked this part because it made them feel like the big kids. I knew it was the little kid's rides, but they didn't know any better. Everyone was happy, and I instilled some confidence in them at such a young age. I packed lunches with Cool-Aid, Goldfish, and all their other favorites. After lunch, we all would get ice-cream. Of course, they had ice- cream all over their faces. We would stay for dinner, and the kid's favorite thing to eat was always string-cheese sticks and chicken nuggets. After dinner, we would all watch the fireworks, and then I would put them in their pajamas, and we would take the tram to the parking garage. I remember when other parents would see me all by myself with three little kids, they would say how impressed they were. My usual response was, "It's all I know." When we weren't at Disneyland, I would plan playdates with other moms. We occasionally visited the beach depending on the weather, and if we were home for the day, the kids would all play together. Simone was like a little mom. She was always looking after Joseph. Joseph would follow her around while Robby would make forts made from blankets. They would play in those tents for hours. Occasionally they asked to make a fort over the TV. I would put that together, and then they would watch all the Disney movies. Every time a new film came out, we would get it. Our house was full of stuffed toys from every Disney movie. Simone had all the Disneyland princesses of course. We even had a dress-up trunk with every outfit you could imagine. Having three young children was a large handful, and at the end of every day, I was fatigued and exhausted. My Phantom's pains were starting to get worse again. I was always losing vision in my left eye, and the numbness in my legs and arms returned.

Robby and Simone stopped taking naps, and Joseph was the only one willing to lie down and rest. I had to devise a game. When Joseph would go down for his naps, the three of us would lay down and watch a movie together. I would usually fall asleep. I think I woke up to poking and noise almost every time after the movie; whether it was Simone asking me to dress her up as a princess, or Robby screeching in my ear like a dinosaur. Yes, I was tired, but my love for my little babies was too much to ignore. The house was either full of laughing or crying, depending on what was going on at the time. Spending time with my kids was all I knew; this was my fulltime job. Every night I would read to all three of them, and most nights, they would drift off into their own little dream worlds, and I thought nothing could be more perfect.

Chapter 36 – The Return of the Phantoms

Life has an odd way of throwing giant curveballs directly at your face as soon as everything begins to settle. My phantoms slowly began to reinsert themselves into my life after a few months of zero symptoms. My arms and legs began to shake and feel sore almost every day. My vision in my left eye would consistently fade in and out. Even though I had spent years with the same phantoms, they still shocked me with how much they still affected my life. I would tell Jenna all the time about it, and she believed me fully. She always had my back, and I felt safe opening up to her about everything in my life. We were always together when Robert was out of town. We even talked on the phone when the kids were napping. Our backyard was being built with a large pool and firepit so the kids could play outside of our new home; it would become perfect for having people over. Joseph finally began to crawl; thank goodness for our very long hallway, it was the ideal practice for the newest little one. The house had become an indoor playground. Robby and Simone slept upstairs where a large game room was set up, so all their toys stayed upstairs. I started to notice that my OCD was getting worse. I was diagnosed with it as a kid, and never paid attention to all my little fidgets and kinks, but the kids had me always fixing and rearranging all the downstairs with their shenanigans. I was fatigued almost every day, and after all the kids were put to sleep, I would crash from total exhaustion.

I had made friends with the other moms from the kid's preschool. Robby went to preschool on Monday, Wednesdays, and Fridays while Simone was going to preschool on Tuesdays and Thursdays. I was busy running around with the kids and taking care of infant Joseph. To keep myself somewhat sane, I pushed myself at the gym to knock out some of the stress. Thankfully it was not even a mile from the house. Baby weight was no longer a worry. The kids were growing up, and they were so happy. Robert's career was taking off at Microsoft, and he was traveling back and forth to Seattle, Washington all the time. He would leave on Sunday nights and fly home on Thursday nights. Weekends would be family time, and Robert was so happy to be back with us. Before we knew it, our backyard was finished, and we could swim in our brand-new pool. It was early September, and the leaves were just beginning to fall, but the heat wasn't letting up; oh California. The kids started learning to swim. In the meantime, we had to put up a gate to keep them away from the pool. During the building of our pool, I wouldn't let them make the pool very deep. At that time, on the news, a young boy was missing from a pool party. The police searched for days, and when they found him, he was at the bottom of the residence's pool. The reason they couldn't see the body at first was because of all the sunscreen lotion blocking the light from peering into the water. Their pool was nine feet deep. This scared me so much. I wanted to be able to see the bottom, so the deep end of our pool is only six feet. I began to title myself as a helicopter mother. I was always worried about the kids. I always thought that something was going to happen to them. My stress was getting worse, but I kept it to myself. I would get up early before the kids and shower. I would stand in our shower and let the water fall over me. It was a time of release before the craziness went underway; contemplation time. I would get dressed and put on a happy face, even though under the surface I was breaking into pieces again.

I would wake the kids up and help them get ready for school. I would always pack their lunches the night before to make things easier for me in the mornings. After dropping them off to school, I would go see Jenna as much as I could. Jenna was always a great person to talk to. We talked about our marriages, kids, and life. I believe that God put my best friend in my life for a reason. I even believe we might have been reincarnated best friends from another season or lifetime. Jenna will always be in my life, for she is my sister. I never shared my problems with anyone else. I didn't want them to think I was crazy.

Chapter 37 – A Frightening Turn of Events

Life was going well; the kids were getting big, and we were settled into our new home. The school was right for the kids and me. The kids made friends while I got to meet lots of new parents and their families. From the outside looking in, everything appeared good. I was able to hide all the pain I was feeling every day from everyone. The only person who understood and realized the state I was in was Jenna. I stayed focused on my family and keeping the house in order. One day, Simone wasn't feeling well. She was four years old now, and I noticed she was running a fever. I called her out of school and decided to get her looked at. Simone was coming down with a cold and running a fever of one-hundred and two degrees. I gave her Tylenol; that didn't make a dent. Her temperature then shot to one-hundred and four, and I wasn't going to wait for an appointment. I called the doctors and explained she was having trouble breathing, and I was unable to control her fever. The doctor said to give her Motrin, so I did. A little while after, she began talking funny. She looked at me and said, "Who are you? I want my mommy". I quaked with fear, I looked at my little girl and told her I was right here. Simone didn't take too kindly to my words, and she started to move to bite me. I tried to calm her down, but I couldn't. She began to cry and kept saying, "I WANT MY MOMMY! GET AWAY FROM ME!" I called Robert to come upstairs to Simone's bedroom. I didn't know what was going on, so I called the Pediatrician again. They told me to bring her into the hospital. I swaddled my little girl, and Robert and I rushed to the ER. During the car ride, I was scared because my little daughter was delusional; she wasn't herself. I retook her temperature as Robert drove the car. Her fever was one-hundred and five, and I was so terrified. Upon arriving at the hospital, they took her to the special pediatric care unit and started running tests on her.

I grasped onto our little girl, no matter how loud she was screaming or biting my arm. The doctor came in and requested they perform a chest x-ray and a spinal tap. I asked, ""why a spinal tap?"" The doctor replied with a possible diagnosis, "We think she has Bacterial

Meningitis." They started an IV drip on her; that wasn't a great idea, because she was lashing at the nurses and trying to bite them. Her shrieks rung through the hallways, and I noticed above the blinding noise. She couldn't turn her neck. The doctor on staff asked Robert and me to step out of the room so the nurse could get Simone calmed down. The doctor explained to us everything they were doing to get our little girl settled and find the solution to the problem. All the tests and the spinal tap came back positive for Meningitis. She had a severe lung infection tagging along as well. When the doctors stated she could die from the infection, I completely broke down. It felt like all my pain I had been suppressing and the pain I was feeling at that exact moment had pulled a trigger, and my cries blasted through the entire floor. Robert held me tight and said we need to pray. We started praying to God and all the angels to save her life. I was not going to lose my baby girl.

We called everyone we knew and asked them to pray for Simone. She was only four years old, and she had an entire lifetime to experience. I remember praying to God and asking him to take me instead of Simone. Four hours passed when they ran more tests on her to see if the medication was working. The nurses and doctors at Choc/Mission hospital were so kind and very supportive. Simons ICU unit room was a clean, isolated room. Robert, I, and anyone who came into her room all had to wear a contagion gear to avoid infection. Simone was distraught when we walked in because she could barely recognize us. They had to give her a medication to make her sleep because she was hallucinating and didn't know who we were. This made Robert and I so scared. We had never seen or heard of this before, and it was happening to our little girl; we felt so helpless. As a parent, all you want to do is fix anything that goes wrong with your child. The hospital had called Father Steve, our local parishioner, to come into Simone's room per our request to help us pray. The virus is extremely deadly for young children, and Simone had the bacterial kind. The test results and her blood work were looking better after all the medication. They were able to bring her fever down to one-hundred and two and kept placing cold towel wraps across her body to control the fever.

After the first 24 hours, Simone was showing improvement. Robert and I took turns staying at the hospital with Simone because we didn't want to leave her alone. Donald was taking care of boys at home, and Robert's mom flew into California to provide any additional aid. My mother and my family in Maine were praying for her. Even our church, St. Edwards, also prayed for her daily at mass. They kept Simone in the PICU for a week. Robert and I were so scared I couldn't stop crying. Between the little moments of clarity, I prayed at every chance I could. Robert was so active, and he kept me sharp. I was living in a hideous construction of nightmares and terror; my own personal hell. Robert was the rock of the family, and he stabilized me at every chance he had. I was so upset and filled with so much anxiety, my fatigue began drawing my own phantoms closer. I kept it to myself and kept praying. I couldn't even think about myself because all I cared for was this little child I brought into the world and Death itself was going to have to claw its hands into my soul before he even touched our daughter, Simone.

As the days passed, she was getting better and stronger. I could tell she was feeling better because she wanted to see her brother's and hold Barney, her emotionally comforting stuffed dinosaur. The boys were too young, and the hospital wouldn't let them into the PICU. Simone didn't like that, and she even told the doctors she wanted to go home and see her brothers and her Barney. This was a good sign; she was, Simone, our little fighter again. She told the nurse, "I want to go home! I need to help my mommy with my brothers, and I want to see my Barney!" Simone was becoming her silly self once again, and I still remember, as clear as day, when I heard my baby girl laughing and smiling after days of horrendous shrieking. The hospital released her after being in PICU for a week, but we kept Simone home from school. Her immune system was still fragile, and we thought it best not to introduce any unnecessary risk by letting her reattend school. When she returned to school, all the teachers and her classmates were so excited to see her. Since she is my daughter, she had to make an entrance like no other; Simone said, "I'm back!" following the most significant smile anyone could ever imagine. After dropping her off at school, I walked over to the church and thanked God for blessing us and keeping our baby girl safe. At that moment, I asked God to help me through all my phantoms striking me in my weakest moments and to give the strength so I can continue being the best mother and wife I could be.

Chapter 38 - Back to Life, and Our Friends

Simone returned home, and all was well. She has always been my little helper, and I don't know what I would do without her. She still wants to give a helping hand at home, whether it be taking care of our dogs, house, or even controlling the boys. I love my little girl. All three of the kids were so close, and school brought them together. They all attended the same elementary/middle school, St. Edwards Parish School. Robby was five years old at the time, and he had a liking towards Legos, Bionicle, and Batman. Robby was always reading and always had stellar grades. He loved school and loved his teachers. He always enjoyed talking with adults more than his peers, but he had many friends; all his friends were just like him. They all played with Legos and were active outside. Robby tried new things when he was in first grade, and we took him out to little league baseball for two years. He made friends, and I made new friends with the moms on the team. He stopped playing baseball when he was in second grade. Robby always wanted to read his comic books, and we would catch him holing up in his room having countless piles of stories he just speed read. He has such an incredible imagination, and always shares his thoughts with me. Robby loved to dance with his brother and sister. They would put on shows for Robert and me in the backyard while choreographing each other's roles depending on the song. I treasured these moments in time; it was so cute. The three of them were always inseparable; they brought so much life to our home.

They were five, four, and two years old; it was like having triplets. I was always running around and cleaning up after them, constantly. My OCD was in overdrive just trying to keep up with the kids. I also cooked dinner and kept the house clean, along with everything the kids did; oh me, oh my. I really didn't understand why I always felt the need to make the house perfect, because there really isn't a perfect home. As far as friends at the time, there were only a handful of mothers, I would talk to at school. I had lots of mom friends, per se, but I mostly kept to myself. I did motherly things with them, but I just couldn't keep up. By the time I was done doing all the household needs like grocery shopping, getting dinner ready, and helping the children with school, I was exhausted. I wanted to be able to do it all and be it all. I kept pushing my body until I couldn't bear any more. I was always falling asleep super early when Robert was home, but at least everything always looked perfect in the house. When Robert was back, he made things so much easier on me. I could fall asleep without worrying if something was wrong. Robert worked for Microsoft in Seattle, and it was hard on everyone. Robert would leave every Sunday night and come home every Thursday night. This was hard not only on him but all of us as well. I can remember crying all the time when he would leave for work, and he would not want to go, but he had a job to do. He was always determined to be the best, and he elevated so fast through the rankings. He was terrific at his job. He missed so many of the little things with the kids during their early school years, and this was super hard on him. Robert is an amazing father, husband, and a loyal friend. Robert 's best friend since childhood is Anthony Bradley; they were born one month apart and grew up together in the same neighborhood. They have always been the closest of friends, and Anthony is more like a brother to Robert. Robert has so many friends all around the world, and everyone he meets always seems to love him. Robert is full of charismatic charm and carries the biggest smile compared to anybody around him. I believe he has always been so successful in his life, and his career, because of those traits. He has always worked so hard for all of us to be able to live a very comfortable life, and Robert would give the shirt off his back for anyone in need. Everyone who ever worked for Robert would tell you the same thing. Robert has sacrificed so much of his own life working to keep us living in California and keep his family happy and healthy. I love him more for it.

Robert and I have had many friends over the years. We even managed to stay in touch with all of them. We never told any of them about all my phantoms; instead, we kept that to just our closest friends and family. A dear friend of mine, Gloria Laub, is one of the sweetest most down to earth women one could ever meet. Our children went to school together, and she had two boys; Derric and Hayden. I loved it when I would see Gloria. She never made me feel like I had to keep it all together, and we would laugh endlessly. She loved to fool around with me, and she would purposely move objects around the house to see if I would notice. I always had to have everything in the house a certain way, whether it be my pillows or a candlestick, you name it. I knew where I put it and how I displayed it. As she walked around the house, she would wait for me to see how long it would take to notice. She thought this was so funny, and it had become a routine every time she would stopover. Every now and then we would have a glass of wine together alongside a bowl of M&Ms. Our conversations generally pertained to our kids. I remember one night we lost power, and all the kids were upstairs playing. Suddenly we both heard the infamous word, "MOM," screeching through the house. Gloria and I went to look for the flashlights, so we could help the kids find where they were going. As they all came downstairs, I would light candles and have the kids sit with us. Sometimes, we would tell old ghost stories to them; we always had so much fun. Gloria would always call on her way to pick up the kids from school and ask if I wanted her to get my kids for me; somedays, I took her up on offer. Gloria is one of those people you meet in life who possess' an amazingly kind soul, and no matter how much time passed, she was always there for me.

Gloria even made Robert, and I order five emergency backpacks, so we would always be prepared for a disaster. Gloria's husband, Glen, was a firefighter in Los Angeles, so they were always prepared to get out of dodge during any emergency. Her van had everything. We would joke about it, but if a state of emergency occurred, I was going over to her house. I knew we would be safe. Not only did we have these backpacks, but we also had an entire shelf in our garage dedicated to emergency supplies. You name it, we had it. All the kids knew where everything was as well. Our neighborhood was always losing power, and that would scare the kids and me. We had flashlights everywhere, and a stock of candles in every room. Our house was ready for any natural disaster.

We also worked together with all our kids to gather clothing from everyone we knew. We collected coats and shirts for men and women. We also gathered buckets of blankets people didn't use or need anymore. The kids even made a letter explaining what they needed and why. The message read:

Dear Friends,
We are gathering clothing and blankets for the homeless and in need, so that they may stay warm during these cold winter days. If you have any size of clothing, you can donate to us it would make all the difference in the lives of those who are not as fortunate as we are. Please call the number listed below, and we will gladly pick it up from your homes.
Thank you,
Robby, Simone, and Joseph Deshaies & Derric and Hayden Laub
The kids gathered so many pieces of clothing that we had to make two trips to the shelter in Santa Ana. This was indeed a fantastic feeling to watch our kids organize

something so meaningful, yet so small in the grand scale of life. We even attended an event at the shelter the weekend after delivering the donations to help work with the team of volunteers. We handed out clothing, shoes, socks, blankets, and meals to so many families and individuals. This was my way of teaching the kids always to give back to their community, and always to help any person in need. Every year the kids would always find new ways to help; the kids and I volunteered during Christmas time the most.

During the summer, the kids would attend one of our local surf academies titled, Ocean Academy. During the week, I would drop off the three of them at Doheny, and they would learn about ocean safety and were taught to surf. Robby already had a couple years of surfing under his belt and quickly became a volunteer/camp advisor. The next year, Simone followed suit and she and Robby would work for hours helping other kids learn to surf. All three of the kids loved to surf and spend tireless hours in the ocean. Joseph never volunteered and became an advisor, but he always attended camp, and he surfed all the time.

My other dear friend, Annmarie Amigleo, is also one of our family's closest friends. Her and her husband, Tony, have two girls, Lauren, and Regan with their two sons, Tanner and JJ. JJ was adopted from the Philippines. We would hang out all the time, and they also attended St. Edwards school. Simone was very close to Lauren, and Joseph with Regan. They even had the same birthday as February 20th. Annmarie and Tony lived in a neighborhood with lots of kids, so when we would go visit, all the kids would be outside running around and having fun.

Meanwhile, Annmarie and I would catch up on life inside their beautiful home. In the same respects as Gloria and Jenna, Annmarie was always there for me no matter how much time passed between us. She is such an amazing mother and a beautiful person. Our children all grew up with strong morals surrounding ideals around family, friends, and community. I always wanted to teach my kids to be well-rounded and compassionate beings, and I think I did a pretty good job with that considering how amazing they have all turned out. All our friends held the same ideals as well, and this helped shape our children's childhood into an amazing place to develop.

Chapter 39 – The New Wave of Neighbors

After living in Dana Point for most of the children's childhood, we never had a single-family live on our street. Azin and Randy were the first families to move in. They had two girls, Maya and Tianna. It was great for Simone and Joseph because Tianna was Simone's age, and Maya was Joseph's. Robby would sit with Azin and me as we had the adult conversations. Azin was very outgoing and lighthearted. She loved to travel, and Robby would love to hear all about her life and her rich history. She came over to the states from Iran when she was just two years old!

Azin had many friends and always had her door open for company. We hit it off as soon as we introduced ourselves. When Robert was on the road, I would visit Azin often for coffee and conversation. Her house was always filled with aromas of the different food she would make, and Robby loved her cooking. He especially liked her basmati rice with chicken kabob. He would even go over sometimes and knock on her door, asking if she had any left-over rice from the night before. Her home was full of antiques, history books, and old black and white family portraits. It was very different from our house but so refreshing. I loved how she decorated, and she would find all her decorations at consignment shops!

We both loved clothing and shoes, as any mother should, so we would go shopping together to many malls and outlets. She always had a warm smile and a heart of gold. Everyone who knew her felt the same way. My relationship was so natural and laid-back with Azin, so I could always relieve stress when merely being around her; that was something I really needed in my life. There would be mornings when Simone and Joseph and I would go over to play, and Azin would just sit with me and talk for hours. She always had a way of making me feel alive. She is a confidant, a spectacular woman, and above all, I get to call her a sister and friend. Azin and the girls lived in our neighborhood for five years, but we always made time for each other. I loved having a neighbor and cherished friend two doors down, but when Azin found this amazing Spanish house in San Clemente, she couldn't help but move. She knew it was going to be her final home, and she loved the history of the house. I was so sad to see them move, but till this day, Azin and I remain close friends. You know when you find a friend who will always be there for you no matter where in the world you are? That description is Azin and the girls. Robert, I, and the kids love her and her girls dearly.

She always comforted me in my hours of need, and I have been there for her as well.

Yazid and Lana were also a part of this new wave of neighbors entering our neighborhood around the same time as Azin and her family. They lived directly next door to our house, but only stayed there during the summer; they lived in Jeddah, Saudi Arabia, for the rest of the year. They had five children around the same age as Robby but were all older than Simone and Joseph. Their first summer living in our neighborhood was hectic for them because of all the moving. I thought they were shy, but Robert and I finally introduced ourselves one morning. Yazid and Robert hit it off, and I met Lana and the kids. They were on their way to Disneyland for the day and seemed to be nice. The next day we all went over to their house, and my kids loved it because they had a swing and trampoline. Yazid was always telling the kids they could come over anytime to play. They had two older children in college and twins in private grade schools in Boston, Massachusetts. Lana would arrive every summer with her maids before the rest of the family. Robert and I would go over, but she was always super quiet. One day, Yazid asked me what my school background was, and I told him that I went to school for art and design. Lana's eyes sparkled, and she and I hit it off right then.

Yazid is an architect, so we started talking about his house and all the possible redesigns he wanted to do. He even asked me if I would work for him designing a new backyard fire pit and seating lounge. Of course, I said yes, because I loved any opportunity to turn someone's home into their dream stay. I drew up the designs, and he approved, and when they left after that summer, I started working on the new project. I loved working on this project for them. I would email him photos as the job moved forward and he would email me back with any alterations or input. This kept me super busy, but I loved it. I was finally using my design degree, and it felt so good. When they came back the following summer, they loved the job I had done for them. They even hired me to remodel their guest bathroom and bring in all new furniture to redecorate the house. Over the years, we all became such good friends. Lana and I started to become closer and closer, and Yazid always loved to tell us his stories from his college years. He was fun and lively as he would say to them, but I would interrupt Yazid and say, "you already told us that story last year." He would look at me with the most nervous smile and change his voice tone and snap, "no, I didn't Steve"; He would do this just to get me riled up. Then we would make joust with our words and make fun of each other. We could develop a comedy show with the content Yazid, and I create. Every summer they would come, and he would always say, "what can I have you work on this year?" He knew I loved to work, and I had all year to get any job done. What better job could you ask for? Years later, Lana and I started to become closer, and I would take her to my favorite places to eat, and we would talk for hours over different cuisines. As we would be leaving the house, I would yell to Yazid, "Lana's going to spend all of your money today!", and he would stand there and try to give me a stern look, but I would just smirk and laugh at him. Lana would always look at me and smile. I loved to play games with Yazid, so I began to scare him. He hated spiders and rats, so I bought fake spiders and placed them all over the house. I would be talking with Lana, and suddenly we would hear Yazid scream. We would laugh so hard, then all I would hear was, "STEVE! I am going to get you back", as tears rolled down my ears from the laughter. Just to scare Yazid every time I was over, I would pretend to hear rats scurrying along the floor, and I would tell Yazid. He would get so anxious. After about an hour of him tiptoeing around his house, I would break it to him that I was fibbing. He would look at me and say, "Steve! You're no longer welcome in my house", laughingly of course, and Lana would say to me, "Dawnmarie, the things you do to scare Yazid are hysterical." Every year I try to find a new way to scare

Yazid, and last year I think I outdid myself. One-night Robert and I came home for a fantastic dinner, we saw Yazid and Lana had a house full of guests. I looked at Robert and said this would be the perfect opportunity to get Yazid. So, I ran to my closet and put on my old camouflage outfit and painted my face black. I looked like a marine about to jump into a swamp and stalk its prey. I crept over our fence between our yards and hid up in the bushes. As I waited for everybody to surround the dining table, I had just designed, I yelled, "HEY!". Everybody turned, and Lana said, "You up there, shut up!", so I yelled back in a blurred and disgruntled voice, "You shut up!". Yazid jumped up and said, "who's out there?", he went running inside, and like a leopard, I leaped from the trees and grabbed him. He was horrified at first, but then saw it was me. I had never gotten him so good, and Lana burst out laughing. The highlight of my summer with them is scheming with Lana, devising new tactics to rile up her husband.

I would go over and sit with Lana for hours almost every day during the summer; she was my sister from overseas. Every year before Yazid and the kids arrived, Lana and I would buy all the new furniture and redecorate their home. They always loved every design I did over the years. One year, Lana and I were sitting out back with Robert and Yazid at the firepit, and Lana said to me, "You know Dawnmarie, I never liked you at first, but over the years you have grown on me", with shock in my voice, sprinkled with a tiny bit of sarcasm I said, "what?", then she said, "Yes, I didn't like you at all, but now I love you like a sister". We all laughed, and after that, we got even closer. Now it's Robert and Yazid against Lana and I every summer; it's quite hysterical to attend.

Another fantastic couple that joined the neighborhood was Miriom and David. Much like Azin, Miriom and I hit it off immediately. She was full of spunk and was always dressed flawlessly; people strive to look as good as she does. Not only was her outlook on life positive, but her faith inspired my own. She and her family were very faithful to the Church, and I loved this about her and her family. Luckily, she lived right across the street from us, so I would stroll over to her house on a bad day. She and I would talk for hours about fashion, life, faith, and yes, gossip ensued. Nothing was held back between the two of us. Even on the toughest of days, she would hold my hand and say, "Sweetheart, I'm going to bless you with my aura, and we can open up some wine to boost our spirits." I remember one night; specifically, that showed me how close Miriom and I had become; a couple of the girls and I went out to dinner. It was a table of my closest friends, so I decided to talk about some of the phantoms that had been haunting me recently. A couple of the girls soon became standoffish as I continued to open. Miriom and Azin, however, embraced me with open arms and took me for how I was. I knew those two friendships stood above the rest because they accepted me for who I was. My favorite part about Miriom is her laughter. Through everything I have gone through, I know I can always go over to her and David's house and crack up about anything. I would always joke with her and say, "Miriom, would you like to go to TJ-

Max and…", before I could finish, Miriom halted me and said, "Oh honey, I'm taking you to Chanel."

Chapter 40 – Joseph, Our Youngest Child & My Increasing Anxieties

Joseph was growing up and doing well. He was born naturally comical and loved anything his brother loved. Joseph started walking, and life became crazier. I was chasing three kids around all the time and tried to keep things together. I made it look like I could hold it all together, but on the inside, I was falling apart. I didn't want the kids to see me in pain, so I started taking a lot of Advil and Tylenol just keep up with them. The fatigue was hard to mask, but somehow, Joseph would always ask, "Mommy, are you ok?"; It was like he could see right through me. I would smile and say mommy is just exhausted from a long day, and he would kiss me and say, "I will take care of you." Joseph was always my little guy, and he loved to tell stories. He would tell us stories about angels and the many things he wanted to do. He loved to watch Scooby-Doo. I loved that show when I was little, so when I found the movies on DVD, I bought them for him. I even bought him all the toys! Joseph would talk about adventures all the time, and state where he wanted to go. We had so many toys in our house that one day, Jenna and I went to Target to buy bookshelves to organize the toy room. This I enjoyed doing, so we purchased four shelves, assembled them all together, and then organized all the toys; it looked like a Toys-R-Us. We even put a TV upstairs for the kids so they would have their own. Once Joseph was old enough to walk, he and Simone switched rooms. Simone moved down as Joseph moved up; the upstairs soon turned into the domain of Robby and Joseph.

I remember this one-day Joseph was upstairs playing with his toys and he wanted to watch Scooby-Doo, so he climbed up on the television stand where all the DVDs were and opened the draws to help him climb up. Suddenly, the entire entertainment center came crashing down on top of him. I was in the kitchen and heard the shattering noise when I rushed upstairs saw and Joseph underneath everything that had fallen on top of him. I yelled for Robert to call 911 because the entertainment center fell on top of Joseph. I was pulling everything off him as Robert ran up the stairs. I picked Joseph up, and he had blood all over him; the TV had hit him on top of his head. I started to put my hand on the wounds when Robert came running upstairs because I was screaming. I couldn't stop the bleeding. Robert was in his office with the door closed, so he didn't hear the crash in the first place. As soon as Robert saw Joseph in this bloody state, he picked him up, and before we knew it, the paramedics were at our home. They took over and placed Joseph on the kitchen counter. They started cleaning his cuts on his head, but they wouldn't stop bleeding. He had cuts all over his arms and face.

The Paramedics started asking Robert and me how this happened to him, and I said, "he was upstairs playing when I heard this deafening noise and rushed upstairs." They were asking Joseph questions, but he wasn't really talking clearly, and he was super scared. Another Paramedic went upstairs the see what had happened to Joseph, he deduced that Joseph had pulled the draws out to climb up and grab the movies. We didn't have the top centerpiece locked to the wall, and it never occurred to me that this kind of thing would happen. When that paramedic came downstairs, he pulled another one aside to talk to him. I didn't know what was going on. I asked if I could speak to Joseph, and they said yes. I was crying and went to hug my little glowworm. Robert was very calm and talked to the paramedics. Joseph was given stitches in his head wounds, and he was super scared. He looked at me and said, "am I in trouble Mommy?", I looked at him, kissed his forehead and said, "no, but why did you pull the draws out?", he said, "I wanted to watch my movie, but you were cooking in the kitchen, Robby wasn't home, and we never bother Daddy when he is working." The paramedic looked at him and replied, "Ok, Joseph, from now on, always ask for help."

We had to keep Joseph awake for six hours to monitor him for a concussion. The paramedic team told us we needed to secure the entertainment center to the wall, so no further accidents would happen. Joseph must have had an angel watching over him that day and thank god for that. As the Paramedics were leaving our home. They gave Joseph a firefighter's hat and stickers and asked him to promise never to do that again. The very next day,

Robert ran out to the hardware store to get all the supplies to make sure this would never happen again. From that moment on, I was a very over-protective mother, even more so than before. I would let the kids out of my sight when I knew they were in a safe space, and I would let them go over to their friend's house for playdates if I was able to stay and visit with the other moms. I wouldn't even let them play outside unless I was out there with them. I thought I was protecting them from everything. I soon found out that hovering over them made them paranoid. I would always say if mommy isn't there something terrible is going to happen to you. Joseph wouldn't go upstairs unless Robby was with him and Simone wouldn't take a bath unless I were standing next to the door. When we were outside, the kids would be playing at the park, and I was always paranoid that they would injure themselves or be kidnapped. My anxiety shot through the roof around this time, and I barely wanted to leave the house because I was afraid of something happening to my babies. I rarely let the kids out of my site. The only place I couldn't control was their school grounds; I knew they were safe there. That didn't stop me from being on school grounds, though, and I began volunteering there. I would either be working at school painting murals in the hallways or working in the classrooms helping the teachers as an assistant. The kids saw me every day I was there. The days I wasn't at school, I was usually with Jenna having breakfast and shopping at TJ-Max. We loved TJ-Max, and she and I would spend hours in that store. We were always looking for bargains, and I was still working on decorating our home. I wanted our home to feel like a beach cottage. I wanted people to come over and feel like they were on vacation. I filled the house with shades of blue, tan, and white. I bought beach themed items and decorated the house as this cute villa. Jenna's great sense of humor helped me control my unbridled anxiety, and she would always make me laugh every time we would get together.

This was a significant time of personal growth in my life. I was struggling with my anxieties about my kids, and all my phantoms were simultaneously kicking in so often that I barely noticed any difference in life without them. When I saw Jenna, we always talked about everything going on in my life, and I would confide in her with my dearest secrets, fears, and anxieties.

My paranoia brought out my fears of Robert wanting to leave me for another woman! This was one of my greatest fears. I couldn't bear to think he wanted to divorce me and remarry. I was terrified my children would be back and forth from one home to another. I remember breaking downing in her living room one day sobbing uncontrollably. She reassured me and said Robert wouldn't leave you because he loves you Dawnmarie. I knew he loved me, but it was my own crippling anxieties that made me imagine the most terrible things possible. I felt like he needed better because I wasn't enough. She would confide in me as well about her fears surrounding her marriage and her kids. Jenna never judged me, and I never judged her. We took each other's pains and worries and comforted each other when we couldn't do it ourselves. I would talk to her about all the crazy shit that kept happening to me, like losing track of time and losing my balance. I would walk into walls or turn a corner and hit the coffee table; it was like I wasn't in control of anything. Sometimes my legs would feel like a wet noodle, and I didn't even go to the gym! The pain would be unbearable most of the time, and I would just go into a corner and wonder why I was so broken. I started to make a list of everything that was happening to me, and then I made a doctor's appointment.

Every time I went to the doctors, I waited for what felt like ages. Once I got pushed through, the nurses would ask me what I was there for, and I would reply with all the symptoms I had written down on my list. I would break down what had been happening to me, and they would always say let's run some bloodwork. Then they would give me a basic physical where they would listen to my heart, check my stomach, hit my knees, look into my eyes, and tell me to cough. They would say all looks great and we will have to wait and see what your blood work stated. A week later, I would get the results, and the doctor would call me and say everything looks great.

They said I was perfectly healthy, and I needed to stress less. On the phone, the nurse would tell me they would be calling in a prescription of Xanax for your stressful days. Well, I have to say, even though I had been prescribed this drug my entire life, Xanax helped me a lot. I knew deep down inside of me that something was genuinely wrong with me, and the Xanax was just pushing it off. For years the same things kept happening to me on and off, and there had to be an explanation. One day Jenna and I were out having coffee while the kids were outside playing. As I was walking to get another cup of coffee, I dropped my cup, and it smashed into a million pieces all over the floor. Following that, my hand went completely numb, and I couldn't even hold a closed fist. Jenna was trying to make light of the situation and said, "well if you really don't like that cup, I can buy you your own." We laughed, and then I started to cry; I was so frustrated with myself. Jenna would be a good doctor because she always seemed to have the answers. She was always looking things up on her computer after our conversations looking for any indication of what might be causing my phantoms. I hated the computer, and I never wanted to use it. I have never been good with technology until recently, and yet I still must ask Robert for help with anything to do with technology. Jenna said she started looking up my symptoms, and she said I needed to go to a specialist, like a neurologist or orthopedic surgeon. Every time she mentioned the bone doctor, I would laugh and say, "I don't have broken bones!", and we would laugh. Jenna would always joke and say listen to doctor Jenna; she knew what she was doing. I was standing there as she was looking up doctors for me to call and I wrote down all the names I could when the list pulled up. I was ready for a fresh outlook on my crazy symptoms.

Chapter 41 – The Car Accident & Balancing Everyday Life

After leaving Jenna's house, we headed home. The freeway was packed to the brim with cars; it was worse than bumper-to-bumper. All three kids were in the minivan with me, and it was a hot summer day. Between the exhaust from the cars and sheer heat from the asphalt, the kids were tired and very fussy. Suddenly a large, white Ford truck hit our van from behind. My head slammed against the steering wheel, and my right hand snapped backward from the way I was holding the wheel; my seat belt didn't keep me back during this sudden and unexpected crash. My knees smashed into the dashboard, and before I knew it, I jumped out of the car. I ran to open the car door to check on the kids. They were crying from the loud noise the crash made, and I looked at the back of our van; it was crushed.

All three of the kids were in their double-harness child seats with their belts on; thank God. The adrenaline was running through me, completely ignoring my own injuries. I was trying to calm the kids down, and I examined them for any wounds. Thankfully, the kids were unharmed, so I called 911. Before I completed the call, I saw squad cars roll up to the accident. The truck that hit us hadn't been paying attention hit the gas from a full-stop, and ran right into the back end of our car. The police officer congratulated me on having the kid's safety-harnessed and told me I was lucky. It could have been one of the worst days of my life if I hadn't had my children secure. The officer then noticed that my airbag didn't go off, and I had a huge bump on my head. I felt my forehead swelling as the adrenaline wore out, and I began to stumble when I tried to walk. The officer said I needed to go to the hospital. All I wanted to do was get my children home and out of the car. The police officer was kind enough to escort me and the kids' home. When we arrived at our doorstep, Robert came running out. Robert took us to the hospital shortly after, where we all got checked for any injuries. The nurse placed my neck in a brace and assigned one for my wrist as well. I was fully mechanized like the bionic woman. The hospital made an appointment with a local doctor, by the name of Ashkenaze, he was an orthopedic surgeon. I saw him the very next day, and they ran x-rays. The test came back that I had snapped my radius in my right hand and had to have surgery to repair it. Literally a day beforehand, Jenna and I were joking that I didn't have any broken bones.

The surgery date was a week out, and my hand was getting extremely swollen. It felt like I had placed it in a firepit, and it was searing from the heat. I had my surgery, and then I was in a cast for four weeks; this was super hard. My mother came out to help me with the kids during my recovery' I loved having her at the house. The kids loved to see her, and she would drive them to school for me. Jenna was coming over a lot to help me as well, and Robert was trying not to travel as much because I really needed help. Basically, having one hand tied behind my back wasn't fun. I was trying to be a good mom and do everything I could. When I was at school picking the kids up or dropping them off, everyone would ask how I was doing? I just smiled and said, I am ok. Jenna and Robert were the only two people I trusted to tell about all the crazy shit that kept happening to me.

Not long after the surgery, my right hand began to feel better; I was happy about that.

At this point, I was still experiencing all the symptoms my phantoms had brought, uninvited as I might add. They would come and go, and one day, it would be extreme fatigue all over my entire body. A week later, I would lose my vision in my left eye again! Black stars began to form in my periphery not too long after the accident. Weeks would go by where I had a giant fog over my head, and I could barely focus on all the mommy things I had to get done. My phantoms struck all at once most of the time, but somedays only one symptom would rear its ugly head. There was no rhyme or reason as to why it was happening.

I thought, "ok, it has to be all in my head. I must be going crazy, or I am just a stressed mother". I continued to wonder why my phantoms would come and then go away for months at a time, and then comes back out of the blue. Well life had to go on, so I just dealt with it; what else was I going to do? I tried to stay positive and keep myself busy as usual. I think I drank enough coffee during this time to fill up ten large swimming pools, so I could fight my constant fatigue; Starbucks was making a fortune off me. We should have brought stock when they first opened, at least I would have millions in the bank by now. Also, I should have bought stock in pharmaceutical companies because they were also making bank off me with my prescription for Xanax.

Over the years, I have broken at least two-hundred cups, from my hands suddenly giving out on me. My left hand was constantly numb, and I couldn't hold anything for longer than five minutes. I started to buy plastic cups and plates because I was afraid of breaking more things. Target really loved my husband's credit card. Every week I was there replacing something I had broken.

I had dropped my blow-dryer and curling iron, so many times I had to replace those as well. I was becoming the mom who dropped everything. Even folding laundry was difficult most days. Robert would laugh at me and say, "Well if you just wanted to buy new cups, plates, blow-dryers, or new curling irons, you don't have to break all of them." Sometimes I would laugh with him because it was becoming a habit. Other times I looked at him with a disgruntled grin because he had no clue what was really happening to me on the inside. I would get really frustrated with him, but it wasn't his fault. Neither one of us knew why this was happening.

On weekends we would take the kids to Disneyland for the day. We would laugh and have so much fun with them; these days always seemed to be good because I never really had any problems. At the end of the long day on the drive home, all three of the kids would fall asleep, and I would too. When we would get home, we would put the kids to bed, and Robert would stay up watching TV. I was always so exhausted, so I couldn't stay awake. I would wake up in the middle of the night, wholly awake and just sit in the living room for hours thinking of absolute zip. Some nights I would start walking around the house for no reason at all. I would go back to bed, but in the morning, I felt so tired. On Sundays, I never wanted to do anything but nap. The kids would want to go do something, and I would feel bad, so we would pack up the car again and go out for another long day of adventures. Weekends were always family time. We were always on the run from adventure parks, riding our bikes down to the beach, or even just driving to Fashion Island to watch the kids play around the fish pound; they didn't care what we did, as long as we were together having fun. We would also go down to Balboa Island and let the kids choose either ice cream or go into the candy store. Each one of them would fill their bags full of colorful candies, and then we would all walk around Balboa. We would take the ferry over to the peninsula once the kids saw the giant Ferris Wheel across the way. They loved this because we would always see seals in the water, and when we arrived on the other side, there was an arcade the kids would play the games in. It was like Robert, and I was chasing puppies; they were little, fast, and didn't listen. Robert's help was always appreciated; he was a textbook father. He took on most of the running around after the kids, and he always brought the biggest smiles to their faces when he scooped them up on the slightest whim. Unfortunately, weekends don't last forever, so when Monday would come around, it was always hard for myself and the kids to see daddy go away for work. I felt pressured to look normal in everyone's eyes, and for some reason, I felt the need to do this instead of reaching out for help. I thought people would persecute me for merely wanting attention!

I was always trying my hardest just to push through the everyday pain and exhaustion. It felt like I was losing my memory, and as I tried to recall simple things, a fog would descend, and my brain couldn't function. I was feeling disconnected from myself and the world around me, it was an age of endless insomnia. Was I caught in a dream? Even when I was exhausted, I still couldn't fall asleep. In the mornings, after getting the kids off to school, I would always need four cups of coffee just to start my day without falling back to sleep. When three 'o'clock rolled around, I would stress about getting to school on time to pick up the kids. I always had to have a happy smile and put on my "mom" face like I had everything under control because I couldn't bear the judgment of other mothers. The parking lot at St. Edwards was always crazy. All the kids rushed out as the bell rung to find their moms or dads. I had to wait in the carpool line to get out, and most days the kids hopped in the car happy. Somedays, they were unruly due to having a bad day at school. I would call those days, the witching hour! I would tell them when we got home to put everything down and talk. The kids would say to me some of the funniest things like, "Mom! Did you know that Suzie did this today?" and, "Tommy yelled at the teacher for taking away his crayon" and, "Johnny was a stupid boy for pushing another kid and had to go to the principal's office." Every day there was always a story to be told. Their principal, Mrs. Rand, had a heart of gold, and she and I became great friends. I picked the kids up in her office at least half the school week. Their stories and excitement helped nurse my day back to good feelings because the kids always made me laugh. Well after everything settled from the after-school craziness, it was homework time. Everyone hated homework, even me.

Robby was good about doing all his homework on his own and thanked God for that. Simone needed help sometimes, and Joseph's homework was easy.

It was easier to keep the facade and pretend I had everything under control, but deep down, I was living a deep and painful lie. I would put that all too familiar smile up to distract everyone, but it began to eat at me from the inside. It was so hard to hide all the pain and depression when in front of my children; I needed to protect them, but my worry outweighed my personal well-being. I wanted to be that mom that had everything under control. That mom who could bake cookies, look pretty, and act like Mrs. Cleaver from the old television show, "Leave it to Beaver." She was the archetype for the perfect housewife; that's the imperfection of our society always to strive to be "perfect." That's who I thought I needed to be.

I know it was just a television show from a long time ago, but its imagery stayed with me since I was a little kid. There would be days when the kids would fight over the craziest things, and that would really push me over the edge. It was a sudden flick of anger that would push through my brain like a light switch. I would fall apart and have a meltdown in front of them after trying my best to make dinner. I wouldn't even eat, and Robby would always get upset at me because he told me I wasn't being kind to myself. I would just go to my room and cry from the fatigue and pain I was feeling. I would always keep it hidden as much as possible from them and just tell them mommy had a headache. They are my children, and it is my job to care, love, and protect them at all costs. I never wanted them to feel alone and unloved because I wasn't feeling my best. I had been living with all these unknown phantoms since I was a young adult, and I didn't want it to infraction unto my children's lives. Over the years, they would come and go as if someone else had control over me. I was a marionette on strings, and the puppeteer was a phantom controlling my every movement. I had to find ways to keep myself moving in a positive direction. I started reading small books about faith and daily affirmations; this would always help. I would always get dressed up like I was going to work, and this sometimes helped me feel better.

My life was a mission of self-discovery. How would I be able to manage my everyday challenges? Have you ever asked yourself who you are and how you came to be?

I know I am Dawnmarie Deshaies; a wife, a mother, and a beloved friend. That was the natural description of myself. I learned how to be a good person since I was a little child. I had always gone out of my way to help others, even when my load was packed to the brim. Helping others has always been a large part of who I am.

When asked to help someone, I would always say yes. Robert would tell me not to take on more than I could handle, but I am not wired that way. I know he was always looking out for me, but I have always been so stubborn, and I never wanted anyone to think I couldn't do it all. I know that sounds crazy, but that's how I felt. I never liked it when someone would tell me, "no," because I had too much to do. Everything felt like a challenge to me, and I was going to succeed. I would push myself to the brink of collapsing, and sometimes I fell. I knew I couldn't do it all because none of us are that strong. Learning about yourself always falls under the jurisdiction of understanding one's limitations.

Fight for what you want, work hard for what you want, never give up no matter want, and above all know yourself.

Chapter 42 – A Series of Nightmares & An Unexpected Blessing

There had been many days my phantoms had stricken me with the most horrible days imaginable. I remember one Saturday morning where I couldn't get out of bed. The kids came to see me, and they wanted to play. The noise deriving from their lips, for some reason, felt like a knife stabbing my brain repeatedly. I let out an intense cry and told the kids to please just shut up. Simone started to cry while Robby and Joseph ran upstairs. Robert looked at me and came over to see what was wrong. When he asked, I couldn't even explain what was happening. I crawled into his arms like a helpless child and spoke, "someone is haunting me and killing me from the inside." I always had a hard time telling him what was wrong, because I didn't want him to think I couldn't be his everything. I was supposed to be his dream, but I felt like I was his nightmare. I was tearing myself piece-by-bloody-piece emotionally and physically. I realized then and there that something was terribly wrong with me. Robert knew it too. He told the kids I wasn't feeling well and that I needed more sleep because I wasn't getting enough. This was something the kids could understand. Simone and Robby would go into Robert's office when he was home, and they would tell him what had been going on when he was gone all week working. They could hear me on the phone with Jenna telling her something was wrong with me, and I was scared. I sunk deep inside myself, and I began to feel I was failing as a mother. I never wanted to play with kids anymore, and they would concerningly say to Daddy, "when you're gone, mommy never eats dinner or plays with us anymore." I had lost so much weight from not eating, and the stress began eating away all my already frail body.

Robert talked to the three of them and said, "Mommy is just super tired, and it's hard on her when I have to travel for work." Robert always protected me and ever had my back, but he knew things were getting worse. I knew, and it was so hard on him to see me this way. He knew me like that back of his hand, and no matter how hard I tried to hide, he could read me like an open book. What could we do? I had seen so many doctors, and everyone one of them ran the same tests, and I swear they all wrote the same damn prescription. Well, Xanax wasn't helping anymore. I felt like all I had to do was just stay busy. I had to keep a positive outlook on life, and maybe that would help. Every day I would look in the mirror and say you're not going to have pain today! Who was I thinking that I could control my phantoms? There would be months where my phantoms pains would stay away, and I was able to stay focused on making a list of things that must get done for that week. I thought planning it out one day at a time would help. I had to convince myself I wasn't Diana of Themiscrya, but I wanted to be Wonder Woman; I wanted to be able to do it all. Somedays I felt so good that I thought I could do it all, but I knew I had to make some changes in my life. It would be best for my family and me. I had to find things to do that made me happy and feel accomplished

I started to volunteer at the kid's school, just like all the other parents. All the volunteers were mostly moms. We would work in the classrooms, watch dutifully over the playground, or volunteer coaching for any of the sports offered by the school. Well, I was never into sports, so I wasn't going to pick that job. Luckily for me, there was another art job that needed to be completed.

I put my name on that list and got the job! When they told me, I was going to help in the classrooms teaching art, I was so excited. I loved to paint, draw, and create crafts with the kids. I even painted murals for any teachers who requested them. Whatever the school needed; I would paint it. The school had a lot of plays throughout the year, so Mrs. Sandland, the fourth-grade teacher, asked me to paint a massive mural of the forest for a play. That year I painted the backdrops for multiple plays, and during the holidays I would create large wall decorations for each classroom door.

Painting always made me happy, and I was feeding my need for accomplishment. I had become excellent friends with Sharon Rands, the school's principal. I really worked for her. She first commissioned new murals in the library; that was so much fun. She liked me so much that she gave me free rein on what I was painting. I would show her images, and she would say yes or no; it was always a yes. I would paint and listen to music, and it made my anxieties go away. I didn't understand it, but I took it for what it was. I would love it when the kids would come into the library and say, "Hello, Mrs. Deshaies!", and they would stare at me as I painted. It was so cute. I truly loved painting and seeing the kids every day. It would bring a smile to my face. I painted the famous Dr. Seuss and all his characters across the entire library. It was full of color, and I loved that I was a part of it. I started to remember all the kid's names who visited me, and I even saw my own children at school in the hallways and during lunch. I think they thought it was cool that all their friends liked me.

Sharon was becoming a great friend to me. I felt like I could talk to her about pretty much anything. When she asked me to paint three extraordinary murals from the Bible, I felt honored. The first mural was a picture of mother Mary and baby Jesus in the garden. It was so precious and beautiful. The painting took me two weeks to finish, and I would work from 8:30am to 3:30 pm. I would listen to soft music, and my favorite song was

"Jesus Take the Wheel" by Carrie Underwood. I played that song repeatedly; I knew everything single lyric and beat by the time I was done. The hair on my arms would stand up as the painting just flowed out of me. When the children would come in and out of their classrooms, they would see more of the picture coming to life. They always had something sweet to say to me, and this brought me such great joy. Over the months, I painted the second mural of Jesus with his flock of lamb.

The last mural was probably the most beautiful of all. I painted the angel, Gabriel, coming down to Mary to tell her that she would have God's son, and she would name him Jesus. I knew I couldn't mess this up. I first drew it on the wall for the right scale and height and then begun my process. I asked Sharon if this was what she wanted, and she smiled at me and said, "yes, it's perfect." I had never been nervous about painting before, but this one was to be seen by everyone at the school. It was at the top of the stairwell, where all the children and teachers passed every day. I didn't want to disappoint anyone.

I cleaned up my art supplies, and before going home to do household duties, I walked over to the church. I prayed for guidance from God to help me paint the most wonderous image I will ever create. As I prayed, I felt like the holy spirit flowed through me. I knew I was ready to paint this mural at this point.

The very next morning, as I got the kids ready for school, I put my art supplies in the car, and off we went. The kids went to their classrooms, and I checked in with Sharon to confirm that we were a go on the mural? She smiled at me and said, "we are all excited to see you paint this beautiful mural for every child, parent, and teacher to see and be reminded of this miracle." I started to paint this mural, and every day, I felt as if the angels' were standing right next to me because I never once felt pain anywhere in my body as I was painting. I made sure every detail was just like the picture that Sharon had given me. Every magical feather in Gabriel's wings had to look soft and angelic, so when I would look at it, I could feel them. I would spend hours on just one feather. When I was done with his wings, I moved to the smallest details of his radiant and gentle face as his hand reached over Mary's head. As I was painting Mary, it felt like she was standing right next to me. Every stroke I made with my paintbrush was in the smallest of movements to make sure she was beautiful and glowing. This mural was a labor of love, and everyone who would walk by me as I painted this would whisper as if we were in church. Even though I had painted many murals in my life, this one was special to me. Not only was I painting one of the world's most famous scenes from the Bible, but I was painting it in the Catholic school where our children went. After three weeks of painting every day, I was finally finished. Sharon came up to see it and gave me a huge hug and said it was majestic and beautiful. I was super happy! I mean super delighted, let's be honest I deserved to be. To my surprise, she asked me to paint the fourth and final commission of St. Edward. He was the patron of their school. She found a picture of him in his thirties, and she wanted it on the wall of the front office where everyone could see it. Of course, I said yes. I began painting this mural three weeks after finishing the previous. This took me four weeks to paint because I had to sit on the counter to paint, and my legs, neck, and back were always fatigued or in pain. When it was done, I was happy with my work and Sharon was to. After that, I took time off from painting.

Chapter 43 – Robby and Me, and our Adventures with Abby

Just as everything was settling in my life, Robby started to get sick all the time. I would take him in to Dr. Jim Sears, the son of the famous pediatrician Jim Sears, to have him looked at. He had been our pediatric doctor ever since we had moved to California. All our children were given their vaccinations at his office. Jim was always great with the kids, and as much as we liked seeing him, it was becoming a recurring event with how much we visited. Robby was always suffering from one cold to the next, and he began to have respiratory problems. I asked Dr. Sears if Robby had Asthma? I told him about my childhood growing up with Asthma, so Jim sent us to another great doctor to have Robby tested for allergies and Asthma. Dr. Marc Dyer had all the test's done on Robby, and his results came back positive for an allotment of allergies and Asthma. He was allergic to everything from grass, flowers, dogs, and cats. You name it, and he was allergic to it. We couldn't believe it. I felt like it was all my fault. Half of Robby's DNA was from me, and most of my family had a severely bad history when it came to medical situations. I grew up allergic to everything, and I had asthma attacks all the time, I couldn't bear to see Robby turn into the broken little child like I was.

Robby began a cycle of different medications just so he could live a healthy life. He was given every day breathing treatments, Prednisone, and we were always at doctors for a checkup. Robby stayed happy, and we did everything we could to keep his life regular. We put a special air conditioner and air filter in the house just like the hospital, so he could breathe normally. We even had all the carpets cleaned every month, so our dog's hair wouldn't pollute it. We changed everything in his bedroom to be allergy-free. He didn't care for stuffed toys, so that was good. I was always cleaning the house regularly because our newly acquired German Shepard, Usul, shed at least ten pounds of hair a day. He had to be outside more often than in because he would flare Robby up. I was trying to keep everything super clean, and this became more stressful on me. We didn't want to get rid of our beloved Usul because he was so great with the kids, and I felt protected with him in the house. I would have to vacuum the house two times every day, so Robby wouldn't have any Asthma attacks. The doctors had also prescribed Robby on Prednisone. He took the steroid every day for weeks to keep his lungs healthy, and then they would cycle him on and off every three weeks. He had to carry Albuterol with him all the time because his lungs could experience an attack at any time. Robby would have to go to the nurse's office daily for breathing treatment while he was at school. He sat in front of the classroom to avoid any of his classmates who might have a cat; he couldn't even sit next to them because his allergies were so terrible. The slightest change in his environment would trigger an asthma attack.

Robby was in and out of the hospital all the time. His breathing consistently struggled, and he was put through multiple breathing treatments a day so he could breathe. As Robby became more accustomed to living in the fortification of medicine, he felt more and more trapped. He just wanted to be normal, much like myself growing up. As Robby grew, his Asthma became worse. Every few days, we would see his doctors, and they continued to prescribe new medication all the time. At one point, Robby was in the hospital for a week. Not only was he in the hospital for his Asthma, but he also had a severe case of Pneumonia. His lungs were riddled with infection, and he was placed on an IV Drip with myriad medications. Don't forget about all the other drugs that had to be cycled throughout his average day as well. He had missed so many days of school, but the teachers always worked with him on making up his homework. Robby was always a fast learner and was able to process and continue working on his schoolwork. When Robby was sick, I always thought it was my fault because I grew up in a similar situation. I believe every mom and dad feel somewhat responsible for their children's genetic makeup, because of our DNA and the family's history of illness that entails with it. Unfortunately, our kids are the product of mine and Robert's DNA, but Robby got the short end of the stick and was given all my family's illness. Even Robert had severe allergies to cats, so at least Robert and I could share the guilt.

Robby was growing up, and he really enjoyed talking with all his teachers; they loved him. Some days Robby would have lunch with them to catch up on work he had missed due to his absences. On the weekends, he would hang out with his friends. They were all into superheroes, comic books, and videogames. He had a great group of friends, and he felt regular with them around. Robby knew how to take his medication when he had attacks, so I felt comfortable knowing he could take care of himself. All his friends even knew the signs of an asthmas attack, so they also knew what to do.

A new and bizarre thing began happening to me. I would get ready to leave the house, and as I would start to lock everything up, then I would run through my mental checklist. As I checked each box, mentally, I would go to my car and start driving down our hill. Suddenly, I began to think, "did I do that? Did I lock up the house? Did I turn off my curling iron? Did I feed Usul?". I couldn't remember if I had done these things from the same morning only seconds after leaving, so I would go back home and double-check if I did. I began losing memory and track of time. I would call Robert, crying on the phone, when he was away at work and told him about my mind unfolding on me. He said I had too much on my plate. That became a regular thing, and Robert suggested going to the gym. I took his advice, and I decided the days I wasn't volunteering at school, I would go to the gym. On the weekend, the kids would come with us to the gym, and they loved the daycare. I made friends with one of the daycare personnel at the gym, her name was Abby. She was terrific with the kids, so I asked her if she would babysit them. She said, yes!

We all loved Abby, and she was my lifesaver. Robert and I could start having couple time again, so every weekend Abby would come over, play with the kids, and put them to bed while Robert and I would go out to dinner or a movie. I treasured our time together, and it felt like I could be me again. I never worried about the kids when Abby was there, and Robert and I were rekindling our flame. It hadn't lacked any luster, but our time together felt like the days before we had kids. We even took Abby to Hawaii with us two times! She was perfect and amazing. I can remember when we decided to take a trip on the road to Hana one year. Let me tell you guys, THAT DAY was a really, really, long adventure. From narrow single-laned roads to waterfalls, and a beautiful natural pool, we saw it all. I would tell stories, as Robert would drive, about the Hawaiian gods and how they lived in the high mountains. I would tell the kids and Abby we had to behave, or they would strike us down with the thunder! Well, the ride was extremely long, and we all had to pee so bad, but we were in the middle of nowhere.

I told Robert to pull over because I couldn't hold my tinkle anymore. On the side of the road, the boys went over to the trees and peed. Abby, Simone, and I stayed close to the car, and the three of us knew we had to pee. Since women aren't born with a weird looking noodle to pee, we all had to squat. As I was squatting, a small lizard came slithering right in front of me. I screamed so loud and ran with my pants still down. I even think I was still peeing as I was screaming. Robert and the boys came running back after hearing my shriek. I was white as a ghost, and Robert asked what happened? I said a lizard came right in front of me. Simone and Abby were laughing, and Joseph said, "Mom, you made the Maui gods mad by peeing in their garden." We all laughed so hard. That is the kind of laughter we all need in our lives. If only we could bottle it and use it at our times of need. As we finally arrived at the waterfalls, Abby took Joseph and Simone's hands, and Robby took Robert' and I's. We made our way down the hill, and it was incredible. We sat down and absorbed this astonishing sight. We had been out in the Hawaiian wilderness for the entire day, and by the time we got back to the hotel, we were all exhausted.

The next morning, we went down for breakfast, and we saw Tess. She worked at the café we got food from every morning, and she had become a part of our extended family. The kids would run up to Tess and give her big hugs every time they saw her. Tess had seen our kids grow up every summer. We had been coming to Maui ever since Robby was six months old. Robby told Tess that same morning, "Mom made the Maui gods mad yesterday," Tess looked at me and said, "Dawnmarie, why would you go and do something like that?" Then all three kids told the tale of their mom peeing as she escaped the wrath of an undomesticated lizard. Tess laughed so hard, and her laughter erupted ours. Yes, I was the only bad one I said. Everyone else peed in the right spots, but I picked the wrong one, I guess. We loved seeing Tess every morning, and we made so many extended family friends in Maui over the years.

Abby was so incredible during our trip. Everyone loved her. She had become a part of the family, and she still is to this day. Since we lived in such beautiful California weather, every summer, we would have cookouts in the backyard with our friends and family. Having Abby in our lives made things so much easier on me, and she was like an older sibling to all the kids. Robert and I would have date nights every weekend, and we would even go away on short trips while Abby would stay with the kids over the weekends. Robert and I could have time to be ourselves, and yes, sexy time was always initiated once we left the kids with Abby. I loved spending time alone with Robert, and this really seemed to help me with all my anxieties. Could it have been stress that made me feel awful all the time? Or was there really something wrong with me?

Chapter 44 – Family, Life, and Continuing Adventures

My mom, Barbara, came out every now and then to see the kids. She lived in Maine and was not in good health herself. She had Diabetes, Heart Disease, and COPD as well, so traveling was super hard. She also didn't like to fly at all. She really missed seeing the kids growing up, and when she was able to, she took a flight out to see us. Robert's mother, Judith, came out when she could, and she lived in Massachusetts. She was working a fulltime job. She also had health problems. If the country took a poll on parents, I'm sure everyone would check off something wrong with them. Judith would come out to visit as much as she could also. Robert's brother, Donald, would come to visit when he could, and he was living in Florida. All our family lived back east, and Robert's dad lived in Massachusetts also. He came out once to see the kids on Christmas in California.

When Robert was home for the occasional week off travel, I would be so happy to have him back. He would play with the kids, and I would have some solo time.

Some days I would just get my nails done, while other days I would walk the beach path to clear my head. I didn't want to tell Robert that my phantoms were coming back, but I was having a bounty of terrible headaches and vision problems. I knew I wouldn't be able to hide it from him, but I thought to myself I had to try. I was trying to be his Wonder Woman. The pain in my neck became so bad that I couldn't even move it than a couple of inches on some days. I would break down crying from all the phantoms on an occasional morning. I kept it to myself, so he wouldn't worry. I began not to eat because it took all the energy, I had left in me just to get the kids fed and ready for bed, and I would forget to eat myself. The only person I told was Jenna until one day, the pain was so bad that I couldn't see out of my left eye, and my left hand was painstakingly numb. I didn't want Robert to think I couldn't be a good mother, so I tried to keep everything in our house together. I tried my best to put on my happy face. My routine would consist of waking up at six in the morning, showering, getting dressed, and finally waking all three of our children up. I would then bring them to school. I continued to do this for years and never told anyone how much pain I was in. It was getting so bad that I couldn't even hide it from Robert any longer. Robert said we needed to see a doctor out in Los Angeles to see if they could give us any answers. I lived with my phantoms for more than fifteen years, and no doctor had ever explained why or how these things were happening to me. Every doctor had the same response. If I had a dime for every doctor's appointment I made or every prescription I had been given, I would be close to a billionaire by now.

A friend of ours told us about a great neurologist located in Los Angeles, so we made an appointment to go up to see this "incredible" doctor. Once at his office, after all the basic preliminary questions and introduction, he ordered an MRI on my neck. He also said I needed Botox in my head and neck to help with all my pain, supposedly it would take care of my extreme headaches and help with my vision loss. I began to have the Botox injected into my neck and head to help with my vision loss soon after our visit. The doctor said all my bloodwork came back great, but my MRI said I had disc degeneration in my spinal cord, and that was causing my headaches and neck pain. He prescribed some pain medication and flexural for my neck pain. He also told me I had to attend physical therapy three times a week for my neck and left arm. Okay, so he solved some of my issues, but he was unable to provide any answers. Notably, the answers to all the other phantoms that have been haunting me for so long. I also visited an eye doctor to give any further insight into my vision problems, but when I took the vision test, I passed with 20/20 vision.

Life had to go on, I couldn't just stand around waiting for the answers to my problems to drop out of the sky. I had three young children and a husband to take care of. Once again, I stayed busy volunteering at the church and school. I also took care of the house and my kids. We had planned a trip with our friends Sally and John Reed for the kid's upcoming spring break. We were headed up to Northern California to a dude ranch. The kids had never been to a farm before, and they loved the idea of going. I had never been on a ranch, let alone a horse, but we were all super excited. Robert and I met John and Sally and their two girls, Hannah and Hailey when Robby attended the same Montessori school in Dana Point. Our families stayed in constant connection over the years, and their invitation was more than welcome. First things first, though, we didn't have any appropriate clothing or boots for riding horses, so we went out to buy everything we needed for this trip. The whole family bought new cowboy boots, bandanas, and a slew of flannels and jeans. We were ready to run the rodeo with how decked out we all were. The day came to a head up to the ranch, and the kids and I were ecstatic. We packed up our cars for a long drive and set off on a great adventure.

The drive was fourteen hours long, and we drove strictly north through the night. The roads were long and windy, and with the kids, Robert, and I cooped up in the car, we became restless. The drive was a very stressful trip just getting there, but we arrived safely. As we pulled up to the ranch, I noticed we were in the middle of nowhere. We had zero cell service and zero electronics; it was a real ranch, and we had just been thrown back in time. It was incredibly beautiful. The cabins were old and constructed from real logs of pine! We had our own cabin, and the Reeds' had there's. We unpacked our things, and the leaders of the camp gathered all us to discuss the daily adventures we would be doing. The kids had their own leader, his name was Shorty; he was great with the kids. Then, we all got to meet our horses we would be riding for the week. We were scheduled to ride three times a day, and I wasn't sure if I was going to be able to ride the gigantic animal. I approached my horse, and the trainer told me his name was Blue. He was an older horse, but he was kind and gentle. His coat was a beautiful mixture of gray and white.

Simone's horse was named Tuff; she loved its name, and she rode that bucking bronco as if it was second nature. Robby's horse was named Ranger, and he was crazy. Ranger was a crazy one to control from the beginning of the trip till the last day. Joseph had the tallest horse on the ranch, and he was the smallest kid of the group as well; it was the perfect match. Joseph's horse was named Will, and he was gentle. His coat was soft and covered with brown hair. I forget the name of Robert's horse, but that black stallion he rode made him look like a Texas Ranger hunting down some crooks in the Wild West. None of us had ever ridden on horses before, so I was a little scared. Shorty rounded up the kids after they hopped onto their horses and they rode off into the woods like a band of outlaws. I looked to Robert and said, "well, it is our turn now," in a timid voice. Blue was breathed calmly underneath me, and I felt safe in his gentle nature. Our leader rounded us up soon after the outlaws, sorry I meant kids, headed out and I was ready to ride. Blue and I got off to a great start from his first step, and although he was slow compared to other horses in the group, he and I had a great time. John and Sally had been riding horses for years and had visited this ranch many times, so they knew what was coming. Robert and I had no idea. "Have you ever seen the more city slickers?", our leader yelled as we headed off into the trails. Yes, our leader knew I was a city girl, and I looked ridiculous on my horse, but he wasn't going to stop Blue and me from having fun. Albeit I had no idea what fun on a horse entailed. We all formed upon the leader's whistles, and Robert formed up behind me while Sally and John rode upfront with the other experienced riders at the camp. I had my new cowboy hat, jeans, boots, and riding gloves strapped and loaded; I was ready to go.

Everyone began moving, but Blue had a mind of his own. The leader behind us told me to dig my heels into Blue's back end to settle him, so I did, and suddenly Blue took off from the pack. Thank God Robert was behind me, and he knew what he was doing. I began laughing out of fear, as Blue's stride increased, and I'm sure you can imagine that I had no idea how hard it was to ride a horse. I kept my legs tight to the horse and tried to keep my ass on the saddle, but Blue's movement made it hard. As we continued a fast-uncontrolled stride, my face seemed to gravitate towards the branches of the trees, and I began to yell out, "branch!!". Yes, it was followed by laughter soon after, and Blue took his rest. I turned around to look at the group I had swiftly passed, and lo and behold, they were on ten feet behind me. I rejoined the group, and after an hour, we took our first stop. I saddled down from Blue, and my ass was so sore! I walked around our stop like I had pants full of bricks, but the fresh air and the mountainsides were so beautiful that I forgot about my ass pain. I was having a great time, but I knew I was going to be hurting the next day. Everyone then sat down with our leaders, and they talked about the series of trails they constructed and how much they loved the ranch. After the quick debriefs, one of the dads asked who was yelling branch all the time, and I blushed as I started laughing. I spoke proudly and replied, "it was me!", so that became my nickname for the week. Lunchtime rolled around, and the kids met up with Robert and I's group. As the kids got off their horses, they all ran over to tell us about their riding and cool stories.

Shorty was helping Joseph off his horse, and once he was off, they both strolled towards Robert and me. When they arrived, Shorty said that Will threw Joseph right out of the saddle onto the trail, but Shorty said he was fine after checking on him. Joseph was a bit shaken up at first but continued to ride all the same. I was scared for Joseph at first, but Robert, John, and Sally reassured me the ranchers knew what they were doing, and Joseph would be fine. It was a tough pill to swallow. Lunchtime ended, and I climbed onto Blue like we had been riding for years together. Unfortunately, Blue didn't feel the same, and he turned and nipped at my leg; John and Robert started laughing.

I looked deep into Blue's crystal eyes and said, "Hey, if this is going to work then you gotta quit being stubborn," Blue gazed back and snuffled. So off we went. I continued to live up to my nickname as each branch grazed my head and hat. This time we rode to the top of the mountain. Once up there, all I could see for miles was trees and beautiful green valleys. The breeze washed over Blue and me, and he jingled along with it. I turned and looked at Robert with a quaint smile because I thought this was one of the most beautiful things I had ever seen. He smiled back. Between the two of us, we knew this vacation was an excellent choice.

As we were going back down the hill, the incline steepened, and my leader came up next to me. She told me to remain calm because Blue could feel when I was unsettled. She told me to keep my legs tight around the saddle, and before I knew it, we were at the bottom of the trail. I was so fatigued, my legs felt like Jell-O, and Robert helped me off Blue. I looked at Robert and said, "I can't feel my legs," so we sat down together, and Robert said, "Wow, Blue really kicked your butt. Your body isn't used to this physical exertion, but you'll get used to it". His smile lit me up like it had done so for so many years, and I snuggled into his arms and said, "I love you." Robert and I sat there waiting for the kids to return, and once they did, we went back to our cabin to clean up for dinner. Once in our cabin, I looked at the mirror, and my face was covered in dirt and soot; earth was in places it should never be. I said to Robert, "my butt really hurts!", and we laughed for the billionth time that day. When I hopped into our shower, the water hit my bottom, and I started to cry. The jeans I had on were loose, and from my inexperience, I wore a thong underneath. Well, now I know why cowboys always have super tight jeans on with long underwear. My ass was covered in welts and little cuts from my baggy jeans. Hey, who was I to complain? That was the experience we paid for, right?

When we were all walking to dinner, Shorty yelled across the field, "Hey there branch! You got some loose jeans. Is your ass sore yet?" I replied while waddling like a penguin, "Yea! Can't you see I'm walking with a loaded diaper?"; one could hear our laughter across the field. Thus, from that moment on, I gained another nickname, loose jeans. The Ranch trip was so much fun. All the kids even got to ride Will, Joseph's horse, across the lake as he swam around; this was so cool to see. After dinner every night, we would watch all the horses gather around, and then they all rode up to the mountain. It was a spectacular sight to see them wild and free. The kids learned to fish, make campfires, sing campfire songs, and play poker. Joseph was the best at poker; I think he liked the stakes.

On the final day of our stay, the camp directors organized a contest for the kids. The kids had to ride their horses while holding an egg in a spoon. Whoever was the last to drop their egg, won the game. Sally and John were rooting for Hannah and Hailey, while Robert and I rooted for our kids. Joseph and Hailey were the last ones standing, but Joseph came out victorious. It was a perfect trip filled with laughter, learning, and ass welts; I couldn't ask for anymore.

Chapter 45 – The Unanswerable Questions

After recovering from my butt-problems, I returned to normal life at home. My Phantoms went away a little bit before our trip to the ranch, and I was excited that they didn't hamper my experience. The weird question I always thought to myself was, "how come my symptoms go away for months at a time, then out of nowhere they start happening for no reason at all?" I knew it wasn't from any lifestyle changes, because I didn't change anything in my life. Everything was always the same, day in and day out. My routine was predictable and easy to manage. Well, as easy to manage as being a mother entail. My depression and anxiety came and went in waves, and I began to think, maybe, it was the lack of sleep I was getting. Shortly after our return, I started to have problems with my urinary tract. I made an appointment with my OBGYN, and the doctor told me I had a UTI. He said it was normal, and he would put me on antibiotics to help. Basically, I forgot to pee after Robert, and I got it on. I always felt like the doctors helped with the easily solvable ailments, but other situations involving more complex illness baffled them; this was still the case in my situation. From that stance, it's always about cycling to the next patient. Then, I started to notice I was having pain every time Robert and I would be intimate. This was a problem affecting me both mentally and physically because I wanted to feel sexy and be desired by Robert. I wanted to look beautiful and dress up for him when he was home. Between the inconsistent phantom pains and the pain during sex, I really had zero energy to spend on Robert. I was falling apart. Robert was very understanding, but I felt like I wasn't doing my ordained job. I wanted to give him the love and support that he needed, but I simply couldn't. I finally came to terms that I needed to find another doctor; one who would make a difference in my life.

So, there I was in my thirties; the prime of my life. I had everything I could want from three amazing children to a comfortable life. I was a volunteer mother and kept myself busy with caretaking activities, but nothing seemed to hit the spot when it came to figuring out what was wrong with me. I began sinking back into a very dark place, and this time, I wasn't sure if I could find my way out. I had thought about taking my life so many times before that it became a regular routine every day. I even thought about running my car off the cliff, so it would look like an accident. Robert would be given the insurance money from the "accident," and he could use that to hire a nanny so he would be able to date and remarry a more perfect version of me; that was my plan which carefully paced through my mind each coming day. Months continued, and it was turning into the birthday season. Joseph, our youngest, was approaching his birthdate and he wasn't looking as excited as years past. So, I checked on him in his room one weekend, and I felt his forehead. My littlest was incredibly warm, and my mom's sensors were buzzing. He had a fever, so I gave him Motrin. Within twenty minutes after the administration, he started to swell, and he kept complaining that his throat was tight. I noticed that his hand and face were blowing up, and I knew we had to call 911; he was going into anaphylactic shock. The paramedics arrived and rushed us to the ER at Mission

Hospital. In the ER, they did everything they could to stop his swelling and bring down his fever. They ran a series of tests, but his temperature was uncontrollably accelerating due to his allergy to Motrin. Joseph had never been tested for any allergies before, so when I administered him the Motrin, the thought of him being allergic to this medication never even passed through my mind. The nurses ran more tests and proceeded to wrap him in ice-cold blankets to bring the fever down. The doctor arrived in his room and told us Joseph needed a spinal tap; they were going to test for Meningitis. Robert and I were so worried, and we told the doctors that his older sister had Meningitis when she was young as well. The doctor explained that there were two types of Meningitis; viral and bacterial. She then informed us that we should pray, because if he did have bacterial Meningitis, then Joseph's life was in incredible danger. Robert and I prayed and prayed; our tears practically flooded the floor. I remember sitting in the chair as Robert was holding our little boy. The nurses prepped for the spinal tap, and they wrapped him like a burrito. The nurses instructed Robert to keep him calm and hold him down. If Joseph moved while the needle was inserted, he was at risk for paralysis.

I prayed to God, Mary, and all the angels. I begged them to take my life instead of my little boy's. I was crying uncontrollably. Robert was remaining calm, but I knew he was also ready to break down, crying from the fear of our son dying. This was our baby boy. We had all been through so much in our lifetime already. Trying to have children was already hard enough. We couldn't lose another baby. He was too young, and he has a lifetime to experience; his time was too early. We waited for what felt like hours for the tests to come back. The doctor returned with the results and told us Joseph had bacterial Meningitis. They kept him in the hospital for five days, and I laid by his bedside every minute of those five days. They kept him on a series of medications to counteract the Meningitis and his allergic reaction. He was allergic to all Ibuprofens, so it was hard to find remedies to help him with the pain and lowering of his fever.

I stayed with him every moment I could, and Robert came in the morning so I could go home to shower then return to the hospital afterward. Five days passed, and he was finally coming home. I thanked God, Mary, and all the angels for saving my little boy. Once we returned home, Simone started to become her little brothers' caregiver, just like a little mom. She was always worried about him, and she forever took care of him. Simone and Joseph were inseparable. Simone went through so much as a little baby herself that now she felt like she was being the little nurse of our house. Simone has always been such a caring and loving girl, ever since she could walk and talk.

She was growing into this amazing young woman, and she always put family first. Well, the path to becoming a young girl isn't an easy one, and her "friends" at that time in her life were so mean. I genuinely mean they were inexplicably cruel and mean. They called her names and made fun of her because she would check on both Robby and Joseph at school. Somedays, she didn't even want to go to school. When Simone was at home, she played with her brothers and our German Shepard, Usul. When she felt alone, she would read to Usul, and he snuggled up next to her in her room; he loved her so much. Simone started to sing at school in the church choir, and her voice rivaled that of angels. She definitely got her voice from her father as well. Her voice inspired her confidence, and she made new friends who accepted her for who she was.

All three of our kids now enrolled in school fulltime. Robby was in 5th grade, Simone was in 4th grade, and Joseph was now in 2nd grade. They kept themselves busy with sports, schoolwork, choir practice, and playdates. They were growing up, our three little babies. When I wasn't working at school or cleaning the house, I would spend all my time with Jenna. We would talk for hours, and I mean hours, at a time about our problems, fears, and of course the kids. Our families celebrated everything together. Whenever we could hang out as families, we took the opportunity. She was my primary support when Robert was on the road working hard to provide for our family. Robert was the Vice President of

Global Networking and Marketing for Microsoft, and he was terrific at his job. I really missed him, and the kids were missing him as well, but when Robert was home, the family was the ultimate priority. He had his mother and brother growing up, so all the time he had with his own family, he made the most of it.

We would plan daylong trips to Disneyland, and we had so much fun every weekend. Disneyland was our happiest place on earth. The funny thing I started to notice was all my laughing and singing started to mask my phantoms and fatigue more so than any fake mask I could ever create. It wasn't bad, and every escape I could create to avoid the exhaustion thrilled me. The fatigue continued, but working out at the gym and spending time with the kids made it easier for me to focus on the positives. When we were all together everything was easier on me. Robert would help with the cleaning and managing of the kids, so we would have time to ourselves. I remember one day when Robert was packing to leave again, and I started to cry. Robby and Simone saw me crying in the corner of our room, and they asked

Robert, "Daddy, why do you have to work so far away?",
I looked at Robert's face, and it looked like a gun had
released a magazine into his big heart. Robert kneeled,
hugged them, and told them, "I work so far away
because I am providing for you guys and your mother, so
we can all live happy lives." I don't think the kids
understood the sacrifices Robert put himself through
because their brains could only process their feelings.
Trust me when I say this, but when Robert was gone, all
he would think about was returning home and spending
time basking in all the little moments. I will always
remember what Robby and Simone said next, "but
Daddy, we can sell our toys, and then you don't have to
work." It was then Robert, and I exchanged glances, and
we knew something had to change. The school was set to
be out for summer break, and every year we would go to
Maui. This was our family tradition ever since Robby was
born. Maui became our second family home, and the kids
loved it there.

This particular year, I remember we were at dinner at our
favorite spot, Spargo. It was located at the four seasons

in Wailea. We had become great friends with Jeb, our server. He was our favorite waiter there, and he had seen all our children grow up over the years. He and his family had become a part of our extended family. At dinner, I came up with a game that would teach the kids how to talk at dinner and carry on conversations while we would eat. I called it, "Guess that Movie." We would each take a turn picking a movie, then we would have to quote a line from the film, and finally, we all had to guess what movie it was from. Yes, it's a simple premise, but it was so much fun. I cannot stress this enough, but we played this game at every dinner for years, for hours. We would even have the waiters join in with us to spice things up.

Sometimes, the kids would change their voices to match the characters they were quoting, and pee always seemed to be a result of the laughter. We had made so many memories in Maui with our family and friends. Maui is our happy place, and every time we would visit, time picked up where we left off. Robert and I would watch as the kids played in the water without a care in the world, and when the late afternoon rolled around,

Robert would jump in the water with them. This was the kid's favorite time of day because daddy would throw them yards away into the ocean and even body surf with them. Summers were always our family's special time.

At the end of that summer, we would get the kids ready for school by shopping for all their supplies. It was always a crazy time because we had to buy the uniforms and juggle the hordes of other mothers assaulting the Staples and Walmart for school supplies. I can remember Robert and I running up and down the alleys of Walmart with all three of the kid's school lists as our cart overflowed with school supplies. This signaled the end of our summer, and our happiness always seemed to fade around this time. Robby was going into 6th grade, Simone into 5th grade, and Joseph was in 3rd grade. Robert's fiscal year was ending as well, and Steve Balmer, Microsoft's current CEO, had Robert selected for promotion on his top list of employees. This promotion meant Robert would have to move all of us to Seattle, Washington to continue working on such an outstanding job. It was such an incredible opportunity for Robert's career, and over the past year, he was featured in every renowned magazine in the tech world. Robert's teams were overachieving the numbers by a landslide, and Microsoft wanted more of his leadership. Everywhere Robert went, everyone wanted him to work for them.

Robert and I talked about this fantastic opportunity and how we could retire at such a young age, but this meant no time with his children or me. Robert turned down the opportunity because he told me, "Our family being together was more important than money." Robert retired from Microsoft after fifteen plus years at the company shortly after. He stayed home with the kids and me as he looked for his next opportunity. He was on the radar for every company out there, and his phone was constantly ringing with offers.

Chapter 46 - Charity & Philanthropy

Robert and I stayed busy, and we started organizing more philanthropy and charity work. Robert and I began hosting multiple charity events at our home every year. We thought from everything we had earned; we might as well help all those in need and help give money to further research on topics of our choosing. The kids were getting bigger now, and I wanted to start doing something again. I wanted an activity that would keep me focused on good and positive things. My friend Annmarie hosted a small event for all her friends to tell the story of Josie and Theresa. These unique and extraordinary twins were born attached to the head together. They shared the same brain! Mel Gibson, the famous actor, and his wife flew them all the way to Los Angeles. They wanted to have our doctors in the state's research and develop a possible surgery for them. So, Annmarie helped organize resources to raise awareness and funds to bring more children who need mending into the states. I will always remember the moment I met Josie and her sister. I walked in the door of our event we organized, and Josie greeted me with the biggest smile. I kneeled to say hello to her, and she looked at me and said with awe in her voice, "you are an angel." It took everything I had in me to not cry from such joy.

By the end of the evening, I took Annmarie aside and told her I wanted to hold a charity event for Josie and the whole organization to raise continued awareness for their cause. I went home that evening and told Robert everything about how the girls came to the USA and how I felt compelled to help them. It was the month of October, and I thought to put together an event at our home for Mending Kids, the organization that Josie and her sister a part of. Mending Kids was founded by Mel and Robin Gibson. Robert agreed without hesitation, and I started to plan the event. We sold tickets and gathered silent auction items to raise more funds for them. We designed the event to take place during the holidays because it was our special time of year. Every Christmas, I put up nine large trees throughout our home; it was a living winter wonderland. I don't know whether it was the holiday spirit in everybody's hearts that season, but we raised over 12,000.00 dollars. The following year we held the same event for them again. This time we sold tickets from October on and had even more silent auction item up for grabs. We also adopted a puppy to auction off, he was donated to us from Russel's pet store. We had a piano player at the front door greeting everyone who walked in, and the back yard was transformed in a ballroom with a nine-foot tree in the center of our yard. The pool had Christmas wreaths floating in the water, and all the tables had long red tablecloths with fresh garland decorating the candles. I oversaw all the work. From organizing the event to schedule with the catering company. We even had live music in the backyard, and two bartenders with the catering crew. They were terrific, and everyone had a wonderful time that year. We raised over 20,000.00 dollars for Mending kids. Robin Gibson was so happy, and Robert and I were so excited that we were a part of something so amazing. During the event planning, I struggled to control my phantom pains, but I couldn't let them down. I ended up losing so much weight by the end that I was a size zero. I was super busy working and organizing that I slept very little.

Despite the pain, I knew our event was going to share so much joy with the organization and myself. I always tried to remind myself about the positives. Every following year we continued to plan events to help other philanthropies who needed help. For the next 5 years, we aided other charity organizations like Loaves and Fishes, a nonprofit shelter for the homeless and hungry. We would ask everyone who came to our events to bring toys, living supplies, clothing or simply donate money for this fantastic cause. We raised over $60.000.00 over five years, and it felt so good to give back to our community. The planning took a lot out of me, but I continued to push through my pain. I believe that the joy of giving back helped me. Every year following one of our events, Robert and I would have people asking when our next event would be. This made us feel good that we could help others.

Chapter 47 – Parenthood; An Up-and-Down Current

I coached Simone and Robby's volleyball team for four years at St. Edward School, and I found out I was a very motivational leader when it came to hyping the team up before their games. Of the many activities that surround parenthood, coaching your kids are always going to be a great time when they are young. I found coaching to bring me great happiness and a little stress, but it was beneficial. The kids were getting big now and going through their own trials and friendships and as a Mother, or Father, I am standing ready for whenever they became too challenged. I was there to get them through their toughest days and lift them up on their greatest celebrations; this is the description of a parent, but it is not set in stone. Not only did I care for and support my children, but I also encouraged them to learn about themselves. This, I think, measures the constant change in my description as a parent. Whatever my children decided to do, I always tagged along for the ride.

At some point in a parent's life, your children start to grow into themselves, and I take it as a sign of growth in my children, but it is always hard to let go of our babies. It's hard to see them walk away and find themselves, but they also know we are there for them whenever they need it. I liked to think that I understood everything going on in my kids' lives around this time, but I didn't. Both Robert and I thought that Robby had it all. He had excellent grades in school and a great group of friends. We didn't know, until many years later, but Robby was suffering from Depression and was continually being bombarded with suicidal thoughts. At the time, Robert and I thought his interest in the macabre was based around his comic books and videogames, but that wasn't just the case. Robby was in 8th grade, Simone was in 7th grade, and Joseph was in 5th grade. During that school year, Robby was rotating in-and-out of the hospital due to his increasingly bad Asthma. One night after staying home for a week from school, Robby came down with a horrendous coughing spell stemming from an Asthma attack. This attack sent his body into seizure-like movements where he couldn't even crawl out of bed. Robert and I were upstairs trying to calm him down when we decided it was time to go to the hospital. Robert picked up our little boy as his body was seizing and rushed him to the ER. I waited at home with Joseph and Simone because I called their Uncle Donald to come over so I could get to the hospital.

By the time I got to the ER, Robby had been sent to the ICU Unit because his left lung collapsed. His heart rate shot up to 215 bpm during an emergency albuterol treatment in the ER, and he passed out from his lung collapsing. This caused the doctors to push Robert out of the room as they tried to steady Robby. When Robert and I were finally able to see him again in the ICU, he looked as pale as death. It was everything I had in me not to cry. Robby looked at me with what little bit of energy he had, and he whispered to me, "I thought I was going to die, mom, all I remember is passing out and seeing the light." I hugged him gently, looked at Robert, and then I began to breakdown into a pool of tears. This was a hard year for Robby, Robert, and me. Robert and I's heartbreak from almost losing our miracle child brought a year of intense emotional and mental stress for the whole family. Robby never got to go to Washington D.C. with his 8th-grade class because his lungs were not healthy enough to travel. He was released from the hospital after two weeks in the ICU. We came home, and we began to take care of Robby the best we could. Little to my or Robert's knowledge, Robby started to sink into himself and lived very secluded compared to the other kids. His spiral into Depression continued to fester, but the mask he constructed hid any signs of it from Robert or me.

Shortly after Robby's near-death experience, I began to have extreme pain in my abdomen. I went to the doctors to get checked out. After a series of X-Rays of my gut, the doctors found tumors all along the inside of my uterus. I was rushed to surgery because the tumors were looking overly broad, and they didn't want to risk them exploding into the rest of my body. Once in the surgery hall, the doctors performed my emergency Hysterectomy. They planned to have me stay one night in the hospital after surgery. Well, one night turned into five days. After the surgery, I continued to have complications. The main complication being my ability to walk; it felt like a blowtorch was pressing against my skin with every stride I tried to make outside of my bed.

I could go to the bathroom on my own, but walking through the pain and fatigue felt like centuries of burning at stake. They kept giving me pain medication, but it didn't even make a dent. No amount of medication was helping my body calm down. The doctors couldn't explain what was wrong with me. Those words sounded all too familiar, after a lifetime of trying to figure out where my pain derives from. Every doctor said the same thing to me for years and years and guess what they said my blood work was excellent and "normal" after the surgery. There was no explanation for all the pain I was feeling, and it was infuriating. On top of my bottom burning from the inside out, I was also having bladder problems. I couldn't pee, and I hadn't had a bowel movement since the morning of surgery. My legs failed to come alive when I tried to move, and I couldn't even walk without help. Everything was going numb; it was like they had rewired me and plugged in the wrong code during surgery. There wasn't anything that could explain what I was feeling. During my last few days in the hospital to keep my mind off the pain, I thought to myself, "well, at least I was able to give birth to three amazing children, so I don't need my uterus anymore. Good riddance periods". It's always better to laugh than wallow.

Well, they finally let me go from the hospital after a week there, and guess what? It was the same routine as all the rest of my hospital visits; they gave me several prescriptions for multiple pain medications and wished me luck on my recovery. Wow, the medication didn't do much, let me tell you, it felt like every step I tried to make felt like a hundred-pound chain-link ball dragging behind me. I tried to sleep the pain off, but even when I was laying down the fire inside continued. Too bad it wasn't a passionate one. The fatigue and anxiety were taking over, and all I could think about was transforming into this scab of pain and fatigue. I could barely recognize myself through the growing fire, and I thought, "Was this the summation of my life?"

The Depression slithered deep into my mind, and I didn't want to do anything. When the kids were off at school, I was in and out of my doctor's office every week. I would sit in the office for hours trying to explain the pain I was feeling, but my words fell on muted ears. At one point, I said to the doctor, "the pain I had before my surgery was better than what I was feeling now," the doctor felt terrible, and I could see her bewilderment. He sat down on his swivel chair and pondered what action we could take to help. After a few minutes of silence, he finally prescribed me a laxative to help my bowel movements and good, old Xanax for sleep. There I was, burning from inside and back to step one.

Two months post-surgery, and the pain was healing at the slowest capacity possible; seriously, it felt like I had the recovery system of a turtle. On the brighter side, Robby was getting ready for his freshman year at Santa Margarita Catholic High School, Simone was in 8th grade, and Joseph was in 6th grade. I started coaching the girls' volleyball team at St. Edward's again, but my endless fatigue made it a struggle. I was coaching the 6th-grade boys' volleyball team as well and had fourteen players in total. We played against all the other catholic schools in the district, and we won ten out of fourteen games. Those winning moments were able to keep my mind off the pain, thank god. However, when the cheering and celebrating soothed, I was welcoming back the pain. The cycle repeated over and over as I tried to remain busy, but the same result always occurred. I would crawl my ass out of bed, put my award-winning smile on, and do what's needs to be done. Deep down inside of me was a whole different situation. I just wanted to scream at everyone and everything; the phantom pains were failing to recess, and I was falling deeper into the black hole of despair and Depression. I felt like I was two people living in one body. There was the mask the world saw and the real me locked behind the safety of my home. Robert worked every day but traveled less. This made all the difference in both my life and the kids. He kept stress off me, and he would play with the kids when I needed rest. What a blessing to have three kids and a husband who helped me whenever I needed it. I began dropping many things more often, and my balance felt challenged continuously. My vision was so unsafe in my left eye that I could barely drive. How much would I have to go through before I had the answers?

Chapter 48 – One Year & One More Surgery Later...

During my recovery, I noticed my breasts were beginning to bother me. I would wake up from a nap, and it felt like a block of iron had been resting on my chest. I wasn't sure if it was my Asthma acting up after years of absence, or something new. How lucky was I to experience all this at the same time! So, I made an appointment with my OBGYN, and he sent me to have a monogram. The results came back with multiple small and medium-sized tumors all over the walls of both my breasts. The doctor notified me they were benign now, but they were growing, and I need to have surgery again.

Almost immediately after my appointment, Robert and I looked for a doctor to perform the surgery because I couldn't bear any more pain. We found Dr. Amy Bandy in Newport Beach. She was the leading surgeon in breast reconstructive surgery in southern California. It had been a year since my hysterectomy, and I was still recovering. For those who weren't there the date if June 2011. These tumors were growing and causing so much pain, and I knew I had to remove them. Was I ready for another surgery so soon after barely recovering from my last one? Dr. Bandy explained the operation to me, and it entailed the complete removal of all my breast's fat to remove all the tumors. I would be left with a chest full of skin and no more breast tissue. She then explained she could perform reconstructive surgery on both my breasts, by putting implants in. From a barren chest, she would graft new muscle to hold a new set of implants. Ladies let me tell you that your body is your body, and if you want to have surgery to improve your womanhood than it is your choice; don't let anyone tell you differently. I have had breasts my entire life, and I couldn't lose them to surgery.

After the fantastic explanation by Dr. Bandy, I agreed to the surgery. The day of the surgery arrived, and I was ready to have these tumors taken out of me. So, I went under, and Dr. Bandy did a fantastic job. She completely reconstructed my entire chest. Bandy replaced all the old with the new and improved, but when I woke up from surgery, I was in unbelievable pain. Bandy said the pain derived from all the cutting and reconstructive work she had to do. I was bandaged up tightly and prescribed hefty medication to keep me asleep for most of the recovery. I was told I couldn't do anything remotely physical, and I had to sleep sitting up.

I had leg high compression socks on so I wouldn't get blood clots from sleeping upwards. It was sleep and rest for the next several weeks, and I was ok with it. Robert brought me home and was sanctioned as my private nurse. Too bad we couldn't enact that fantasy, oh well, that would have to wait for another time. As soon as he placed me into bed, the pain medication knocked me out. The very next day, I had to go to the doctor's office to be checked, and I was an emotional wreck. When she took the bandages off, I cried from the pain. I had one breast a little higher than the other, but Dr. Bandy said it would drop in time. My right side was more top because of all the extra work she had to do from the increased tumor count. It was so painful; I was incredibly fatigued, emotional, and I felt like I had just lost a piece of myself. Robert took me home after our appointment, and I started to cry on the way home. I was getting myself so upset because I felt "changed." I wasn't thinking right as the depression rooted deeper, and I thought I would never be the same.

After a week of stress, no sleep and constant pain all over my body, I caught myself looking in my mirror. Who knew new breasts could change an appearance so much. I was doing what Bandy told me to do, and I had to massage them every day. Doing so would cause my right breast to drop and be even with my left side. I was obsessing too much over my physical appearance because I was uneven. I knew it would get better with time, but sometimes we don't have the patience to wait. I wasn't moving forward, and I felt still in time. I was making our bed one day and accidentally pulled my stitches' in my right breast. The sudden pain shocked me, and I called Bandy. She told me to go right into her office to get it fixed. She re-stitched me with medical tape and told me no more household duties. I needed time to recover from all the incisions, and being a mother would have to wait.

I couldn't even perform my essential responsibilities, but I needed to focus on myself after this major surgery. I told Amy about the increasing burning sensation in the right breast, and she was so kind and said, "Dawnmarie, you have been through so much. Your body just needs to heal for once. Allow yourself to relax and forget about all the chores that need to be done". How could I forget to do such routine chores after years of repetition? The troubles of remaining still. The next day I went to see Jenna, and I told her all the crazy things I had been feeling. I told her about my stitches tearing and how my appearance was causing me distress.

Jenna may not be blood, but she is my true sister and best friend, and she said, "Dawnmarie, you're beautiful the way you are. If you feel comfortable to let's call the doctor and I will go with you". I called Bandy then and there, and Jenna and I went to her office. She examined me after Jenna's proposal and prescribed me Levaquin. She noticed I had a staph infection and needed to be placed on 1000 milligrams, twice daily. I went home, took my medication, and got into bed. That day the Simone and Joseph walked home from school. We lived less than a half-mile from the school, and they were old enough to walk by themselves. That didn't stop my motherly instinct from worrying, though. Robby was a freshman in high school, and he got a ride home. Robert was working in San Diego that day, and I wasn't allowed to drive at all. My dear friend, Sharon Rands, sent me flowers to cheer me up. I felt blessed to have so many people praying for me. This gave me some comfort.

My friend Gloria drove the kids' home from school for a week, because I couldn't turn a steering wheel and the medication was too strong to drive. Simone and Joseph would get home from school, and Simone would go outside with our dogs on the front lawn. Usul was our German Shepard, and Gaston was our new little puppy; she would always sit with them and play or do her homework. I could always count on Sim to perform all the caretaking activities for me, my beautiful little helper. Joseph and Robby were upstairs also doing homework. I went outside and talked to Simone. She has always been the sweetest little girl who was becoming a beautiful young woman. As I stepped out from our front door, I couldn't help but admire what Robert and I created. I approached her, and I told her I had to go check on my stitches. She said, "ok mommy, do you need me to do anything around the house?", with a content smile. It was a moment of relief, and I basked in it. Robert and I shared everything with our children. Our family had been built on honesty and openness, and we always talked as a family unit. Robert and I opened a discussion about my surgeries. We then explained to the kids the increased chores that needed to be done throughout the house during my recovery. The kids were more than willing to help their mother, and I was relieved.

As I was going into the house, my neighbor Denise, saw me and said she was praying for me. She was always so kind and loving to our family. I went to my bedroom, closed the doors, and took off my bandages. I had to put the antibiotic cream on my stitches to rid myself of the staph infection when suddenly I heard loads of screaming. I thought that it was Denise's son playing in the backyard with friends, then I listened to the front door open. Simone entered, shouting, "Mom! Tank (Our neighbor's large Pitbull) got loose and came after me. He attacked Gaston and Usul", she was so scared, and I ran outside.

All my neighbors were out front, and Denise's daughter, Reagan, and her boyfriend stopped Tank from attacking Simone. Usul, on the other hand, was fighting back to protect Simone. Tank bit Usul in the belly, and Usul bit Tank in the neck. Simone ran to break them up, but both the dogs caused her to start crying and screaming. Denise, Simone and I managed to pull Usul off, and Reagan and her boyfriend held Tank. We placed the dogs safely into our house while Reagan and her boyfriend saw the woman that was supposed to be taking care of Tank. They told her how he attacked my daughter and dogs.

Denise had me call animal control, and they came to our house to take all our information. The adrenaline was still pumping through me, ignoring my health completely, and we had to take Usul to the vet. His wound was bleeding, and he needed stitches. I was not only scared about my daughter Simone, but also about our family's gentle protector. Simone put her terror aside and assisted me with getting Usul into the car. I was worried about her dealing with the trauma, but she pushed through like the fighter she was. Robert arrived home shortly after, and we told him everything that had happened. He then walked over to our neighbor's house, the owners of Tank, and a woman answered the door. She said she was watching the dog and he got loose, Robert told her to have Ryan call us as soon as possible. The animal control employee wrote up an incident report on both the dog and his owner. Simone was coming down from her adrenaline and the shock settled in. Robert moved to comfort her and said she was a hero for handling the situation the way she did, and she should be proud.

I went into my bedroom shortly after my own adrenaline had settled. A breakdown ensued, and I was shaking uncontrollably. My vision started to phase from concentration, and the pain shackled my body into bed.

It felt like a dark hand had come down and trapped me in its grip. Extreme pain pulsated across my body as my legs and my arms numbed to a halt. I couldn't stop crying. Robert came in and sat down next to me. He told me everything was going to be ok and I said to him, "it was my fault I wasn't there to protect our daughter. I was in the bathroom checking my stitches..." before I could finish rambling, Robert said it wasn't my fault. He said there wasn't anything I could do, but I still felt like I was the worst mother ever. Robert said I needed sleep and that he promised to take care of our kids. I took my medications and drifted into a sobbing haze.

When they came home from the veterinarian and dinner, I was still so upset that I wasn't there to protect my daughter. Robert told me to stop obsessing over it, and I needed to focus on self-healing. The next night Robert and I with all three of the kids went out to dinner. I still had all my bandages on and wasn't driving due to all the medication. That night at dinner Robby, Simone and Joseph had so many questions about everything that had happened since my surgery. Robert did most of the talking and explained my breast surgery; I was still dazed from the abundance of medication I was on. Robby said I was like Lara Croft? I looked at him, and I said, "what?", he replied, "Angelina Jolie just had the same surgery; a double mastectomy." Angelina's surgery was because she carried specific cancerous tumors in her breasts and had to have them removed. I didn't carry the same cancerous cells, but I giggled from the comment because Robby knew Lara Croft was one of my favorite heroines. He always knew how to cheer me up whenever I was stressed. His smile and bear hugs made my world better every time.

Well, it had been a crazy year and two surgeries. Both surgeries I was still recovering from, and Robert and the kids worked double-time to make my life easier. Unfortunately, my sadness wasn't silenced by help. I was always sad, and I felt like I had, I had lost my sexual identity. I began to fear intimacy with Robert because I wasn't sure what my body was anymore. It all felt foreign. Anxiety and depression rose to an ugly surface, and the physical pain continued to wreak havoc. My phantom's grip enthralled my entire body. It was a challenging time in my life. I was full of self-doubt and feeling hopeless. It had been two weeks after my surgery, and Robert took Simone and Joseph out to dinner. Robby stayed home with me. He was always my little protector and very intelligent. Robby had gone through so much trauma as a young child, and he resonated with my pain. Robby stayed home with me frequently, and even though I was struggling with understanding myself, I knew I had done my job as a mother by raising an amazing and caring son.

Chapter 49 – A Shocking Revelation

Eight weeks after my surgery, normal life carried throughout the house. Robby had made plans to go to the movies one night, and he asked me to drive with him. He was taking his driver's education class at the time and had his permit. I said I would let him drive there and I would drive home. I knew I shouldn't be driving at the time from the medication, but I didn't want Robby to miss out on going out with his friends. I didn't tell Robert, and Robby and I drove the back roads all the way to the theaters in Aliso Viejo. By the time we arrived, my nerves were in overload, and I was so anxious to have him stop the car. As we entered the plaza, I said just stop near the curb with a fire hydrant. Robby hugged me and said thank you as he ran from the driver's seat. As I stepped out of my car from the passenger side, my right leg was fragile, and my left foot stepped down on top of the cover of a fire hydrant. The lid moved, and my foot fell in the hole, and the rusty cover cut my foot right to the bone. Robby was already inside the theater, and I was screaming from the searing pain. I didn't have any water or medical supplies to cover or wrap my foot. Blood was everywhere, and I called Robert crying. He told me to drive slowly, and he would meet me at home. On the way home, I was shaking and bleeding all over the floor of the car. I almost hit another vehicle trying to wrap my head around how stupid I was. By the time I got home, I couldn't control my emotions and the blood and tears mixed. I placed my foot in the tub and cleaned it out; the water made it even more painful.

As water flowed over the wound, I could see my bone. I called my neighbor, Carol. She was a doctor, and she came over to look at me and said I was going to need to go to the ER and get stitches. Robert and Joseph took me to the hospital while Simone stayed home. By the time we got to the hospital, it had been over an hour since the accident. The ER in Laguna Beach took me in, cleaned out the cut, and stitched me up. They said we are going to put me on another series of antibiotics when I told them I was already on Levaquin. I explained my staph infection from the breast surgery I had just had, and they said with that in my system already I would be fine. They administered a hepatitis shot because of the rust, and they finished bandaging me up. They gave me a walker because I couldn't use crutches due to my breast surgery. I couldn't walk on my foot for two weeks. When the doctor asks a patient on a scale of one to ten how their patient is feeling, let's just say I was feeling an eleven. I was being held together by stitches and medication; if it weren't for Robert and the kids, I wouldn't know what to do with my being. Was I just a burden on everyone? Well, my routine had been fundamentally changed from that moment, and I was a completely different person. I was the patient instead of a mother. The doctors told me to keep my foot elevated and explained everything that needed to be done to help my recovery. Robert, the best nurse ever, got the bed together in the proper situation, arranged all my medications, and placed all the essentials next to my bed like clockwork. I had pillows behind me to support my back and keep my breasts elevated. I also had pillows under my legs to keep my foot elevated as well. I was the state-puff marshmallow man of pillows.

The very night, I woke up from a nap around two in the afternoon and started screaming in pain. It felt like someone had doused me in gasoline and set me to flame. We called the hospital, and they said it was due to the trauma my body had gone through. Robert and I looked at each other, and we knew something was wrong, so Robert gave me Tylenol every two hours and rotated Advil in every additional hour. All of that was on top of the pain medication I was already on. The next morning, I was in unbelievable pain; it felt like I was trapped in a blaze, and I couldn't breathe from the lack of oxygen. I thought to myself I should just take all the pills by my bedside and end my misery. I wondered if that was what it was going to take to rid myself of my phantoms. I knew that suicide wasn't the solution, and I started to pray for strength to get through this. My body continued to bloat, and Robert saw my increased inflammation as I laid there in endless torment. Robert took me back to the hospital, and he feared the worst. I was incoherent from the drugs in my system, and by the time we arrived, I seized from the mental shock and was rushed into the ER. As they laid me on the bed, the nurse began to take off the bandage around my foot. It was incredibly swollen, and green puss was flowing out of my stitches. Through the lucid haze, I began screaming. It took Robert and two nurses to hold me down to get the stitches out. They took a sample of the green excrement and sent it to the lab. Then they poked my arm and gave me an intravenous pain medication drip to relax me. To control the pain, the doctors gave me Vancomycin and admitted me into the hospital. They placed me in quarantine because the results came back positive with MRSA. This infection was possibly fatal, and the doctors would potentially have to amputate my leg. They wouldn't even let me see my own kids. Legions of doctors and nurses, covered entirely in hazmat gear, flowed in and out of my room. I had special breast surgeons checking on me, and I was also assigned a specialized team of doctors to clean out my wounds on my foot. I had a catheter in it because I couldn't walk, and I was running a fever.

I was becoming a case study for all the doctors. The pain continued to spread like wildfire, and the hospital called our priest. Father Steve came into my room to administer my last rites and final communion. I thought this was it, I am going to die alone, afraid, and lost in the hospital. Unfortunately, I was abandoned by any possibility of peace. I had to be transferred from Mission in Laguna to Mission Viejo. Once we arrived at mission, the specialized team performed a bone scan on my leg to see if the MRSA spread into my bone. If the test returned positive, they would have to take my leg. I was all alone, and fear swept through my body like a plague. The doctors and nurses did everything they could to make me feel comfortable, but they were not my family. I wanted Robert and my children. Somewhere between three to four hours had passed, and the doctors had performed all the tests needed without me being conscious. They returned me back to the Laguna hospital and placed me back into quarantine. They finally gave some good news when they said I wasn't going to lose my foot. They had to keep the IV drip of Vancomycin and another medication because this was the last and only medication, I could receive to save my life from the infection. After dazing in and out of consciousness for an unknown amount of time, I remember the hospital sent a psychiatrist to come and see me. He started asking me lots of questions; he asked if I had ever thought about taking my life. I didn't answer him honestly because I thought they would put me in an institution and take me away from my family. I lied and said no. I did tell them I was extremely anxious, depressed, scared, and had pre-cognitive thoughts of taking my life. I was so afraid and felt like I couldn't take it anymore. The doctors were so kind and caring, and my nurses kept telling me I was strong; I was going to get through this, I am Wonder Woman. They had to keep taking blood work from me every four hours to make sure the medication was shutting down my kidneys, so the MRSA couldn't travel further into my body.

After three days in quarantine, they finally let me have visitors. I had so many doctors on rotation I couldn't keep their names straight. Thank God for Robert; he was my husband, my hero, my savior, my rock, and his love never gave up on me. My dear friend, Annemarie, was at the same hospital because her father was admitted for health reasons and found out I was in there too. She came in and made me laugh. She said, "well Dawnmarie if you really needed all this attention you could have just called." I laughed so hard that it really hurt, but it was the best medication I needed. After a week in quarantine, they sent me home with the walker. They put me on house arrest, and Robert wouldn't let me leave the house. All my friends came to see me instead, and Robert knew I was happy to see visitors. I was being flooded with love now instead of pain and terror; it was a relief. About three days after being home, I was in bed trying to rest with my leg up, and my breasts still wrapped and in a support bar super tight to keep them healing.

I also had to clean my foot with this unique substance containing silver. I also had to clean my breasts the same way. The silver helped stave off the infection. Robert helps me with everything. He would help me off the bed, he administered my medication, and then helped me get back into bed. Robert was meticulous and kept a list of all prescriptions and dosages next to my bed. He would get me settled, kiss my forehead every time, and say, "I love you, Dawnmarie," I smiled and said, "I love you too". Love is such a powerful motivator to heal, it's incredible to see the little ways it works. Love truly transcends all basic understanding.

Around one hour later, I woke up and I couldn't see out of both eyes, and my body was completely paralyzed. My body tremored as I tried speaking. It took everything I had to scream, and I couldn't; I felt like I was in a horror movie, and I was about to meet my perilous demise. Robert came in from hearing this muttering sound I was making, and he could see that I was paralyzed. Robert called all the doctors immediately, and I was brought back to the hospital. Now they had a team of neurologists and cancer doctors looking at me. For the next six months, I was in and out of the hospital. I rotated through at least twenty doctors and tested more times than I could remember. Conclusions finally decided to roll onto the table. It is wasn't cancer, it wasn't more tumors, and it wasn't neck problems; although they did find a benign tumor on the back of my neck and told me not to worry.

I saw three new neurologists over a six-month timeframe, and they all said I was just stressed out from all the trauma. My recovery now exceeded a year, and I stopped wondering about conclusions to my phantoms because no one on this damn planet could figure out what was wrong with me. Each new neurologist made me feel more and more hopeless as my bloodwork came back "normal." I went to see Dr. Amy Bandy for a nine-week checkup after my breast surgery. I trusted her with my life, and I knew she would tell me what she thought when it came to my file folder worth of bloodwork and test results. She agreed with my hypothesis and thought that there was still something they hadn't found yet. From that point on, Dr. Bandy was becoming a dear friend, and she would listen to me. She never made me feel like I was crazy, nor did she ever dismiss me for the next patient. My breasts were finally beginning to look good, and they were healing well. There was a slight boost of confidence there, but I was still unable to be intimate with Robert. I confided solely to my inner circle around this time. That consisted of Robert, Jenna, Azin, Amy, and Sharon. I felt it best to stay close to home. At this point, Simone was going to Washington DC with her 8th-grade class and graduating from St. Edwards. She was about to embark on her freshman year and was going to join Robby in high school at SM. Robert suggested that I go see Dr. Ashkenazi to ask his opinion on my phantoms since he was such a terrific surgeon after my wrist surgery. I went to his office and asked if I ever had ant nerve testing performed. I figured my immune or nervous system must be where all my pain must be coming from since my body always fell asleep and weak. He asked if I had my MRI's done at Mission Hospital, and I said yes. Then he asked to look at them, so I signed the papers, and he pulled up all my reports. He had every MRI I had taken over the last six months, and he pointed out these peculiar white spots spotted around my brain from the MRI scan. Ashkenazi knew he wasn't a specialist in this field, but he believed me when I described all my phantom symptoms and sent me to a colleague for further examination. Ashkenazi suggested that I mention a disease named Multiple Sclerosis to his colleague, who was one of the best neurologists around; her name was Dr. Caroline Choan.

Ashkenazi pulled some favors for Robert and me, since he was a family friend, and set us an appointment for the earliest date.

Two days later, Robert and I were on our way to her office, and we brought in all my MRI's, body scans, bone scans, and bloodwork from the past year. Any medical history we found from this past year, we brought. The nurse put us in the room as we waited, and I said to Robert, "if she doesn't find anything wrong with me, then I am done with doctors." Dr. Choan walked into the room and first thing she said was, "I looked at all of your paperwork, and from what I can see it looks like you have Multiple Sclerosis", she continued, "so, Dawnmarie, tell me the first time you started to notice anything different in your life". I laughed and asked how far back should I go? She replied, "as far as you can remember." I looked at Robert and said, "you ready,"? I started to tell her about my early twenties when I began to suspect something was wrong, then for the next two hours she asked me questions, and we answered them. When we left the office, she said she wanted to perform her own MRI, bloodwork and a spinal tap. This was the first time a doctor had provided me with so much information that I felt encouraged we were moving in the right direction. She was so kind and intelligent; I knew she would help me find answers I had been searching for years. As we both left the office, Robert and I talked about how in-depth she was, post-interview. I told Robert, "I know she can help me, I can feel it." My attention was grabbed as soon as she mentioned my late childhood and early adulthood. Choan had discussed almost every significant life moment with us, and I was incredibly happy to share. We arrived at the hospital for Choan's tests, and I signed in while they set me up for the tests. As they were getting me ready, all the nurses kept telling us how incredible Dr. Choan was. This made both of us feel confident and assured we would finally be getting to the bottom of this. After my MRI, they brought me back to the room to prep me for the spinal tap. They gave me a muscle relaxer, and this medication made me so silly. I began laughing and making jokes, and I tried to remember the last time I was this happy to be at the doctors. It was the first time in my entire life I felt good to be in the hospital. The doctor performing the test was so lovely as they took me into the room. I said, and they rolled me in, "it looks like a morgue in here guys, what are you trying to do? Are you trying to rattle my bonessssss", I started laughing and said, "Gotcha, I'm not dead yet," and the doctor even laughed. In the room, there was a metal table and a lager X-Ray machine above the table. An old TV was also connected to the metal table, and I asked, "am I going to watch a comedy movie? ", and the doctor said if you want to. The doctor then said the TV was for him to see where the needle is inserted into my spine, and I was so intrigued I couldn't help but to watch. The nurse got me on the table, and he asked if I was afraid of needles, I replied, "no! I have been a lab rat my entire life", he chuckled and said, "well did we will help you find your answers?", I let out a big laugh and said, "Yes! Finally,". They gave me more medication in my IV to keep me even more relaxed. The doctor was prepped, and he asked, "are you ready?" I replied, "are you"? They placed me on the metal table face down, and I turned my head so I could see the TV screen. It was so cool; I could see the interior of my spinal cord! They put something on my back and began the operation. I felt a push into my skin, and then I could see the needle going into my spinal cord. I thought this is so flipping cool! It felt strange, and then he said, "I am pulling out spinal fluid," I said, "ok." As he pulled the tube out of the needle, I asked, "is it normal if I can't feel my legs right now?", he replied, "no, you should feel them." Then he moved the needle, and suddenly, I could feel my legs again. He assured me everything was going well and that he needed one more tube of fluid. I said, "ok, I'm not going anywhere." Before I knew it, he was done, and they taped me uptight. As I was getting back on the bed, Robert was there, and I said that was the coolest thing ever. I got to see my spinal cord on TV. Robert looked at the male nurse and asked if I was ok? Then he laughed and said, "is your wife always this funny?", Robert laughed and said, "yes, sometimes she says the funniest things." Soon after the operation, I had the biggest migraine, and the nurse said it was a result of the removal of fluid. They gave me medicine to relax, and I passed out. Six hours later, they woke me up and asked how I was feeling? I said my head really hurt, and my lower back was in pain. They kept me for two more hours then sent me home. I had to stay in bed for the next 2 days, and I had to drink lots of water. After a couple of days, I was feeling my normal self.

Chapter 50 – The Unforgettable Truth

It took two weeks for all the tests to come back with results. Then, we finally had our follow up appointment with Dr. Choan. As Robert and I were walking into the office, I had an overwhelming feeling rush over me. I felt like I had been touched by an angel, and I knew my questions were going to be answered finally. We sat down in her office, and she asked how I was feeling. I replied anxiously, "I am ok, and I am hoping you can finally tell me what is going on with me." Robert was so nervous, and Choan said all the tests came back with promising conclusions. My spinal tap and MRI indicated lesions all over the right and the left side of my brain. So, there was the answer, I was diagnosed with Multiple Sclerosis. After years of wondering what was wrong with me, I finally smiled. Now I know what you're thinking, how in the hell would I be happy to discover that I have this disease? Well, let me tell you. I finally had a fantastic doctor diagnose me accurately, and now I would be able to move on with this chapter in my life and begin a new track to create a new life. It was a rebirth in both my soul and mind. I looked at Choan with a smile and asked, "ok, so what do we do next"? My phantoms finally had a name, and they were no longer an invisible enemy. Validation at last.

Across from me was Robert; he started crying almost immediately after the words, "multiple sclerosis" fell out of Choan's mouth. Robert performed secondary research about the disease before the meeting, and I was clueless about the reality of the diagnosis. We both looked at Choan with completely different reactions, but we were both heading down the same road. After my inquiry about treatments, Choan jumped in an began discussing all the possible outcomes the disease can produce. See the thing is, MS is a progressive disease, and each individual diagnosed is entirely different from the other. The symptoms of the disease remain the same amongst every individual, but the progression of the disease depends entirely on the environment, genetic makeup, and lifestyle one chooses to live. Robert asked Choan if the condition was curable, she replied, "no." I reached for Robert's hand, and I felt his heart sink in his chest. My elated expression was still protruding from my face, and I gripped Robert's hand harder than I ever had before. I looked to Choan and asked, "ok, since it isn't curable what treatments are available for me to continue living my life the way I want to?", she replied, "there are so many treatments out there, mostly pharmaceutical though. From all the patients I have placed onto the medications, most vary in results". I looked at Robert, and from there, we asked if she could name each primary medication and the side effects that come along with them. She began with Copaxone and Avalox, both were interferon injections that most MS patients took. Robert and I decided it would be best to do our own research and get back to her in a week on the selected treatment. We thanked Choan for her incredible and in-depth information she provided, and we said we will be seeing you soon.

On the way home, Robert held my hand the entire drive. We began talking, and we both thought it was an excellent decision to do our own research on each medication before jumping into the unknown. My entire life had been filled with endless prescriptions, and I never once investigated each of the drugs carefully. When it came to this disease, we knew we would consistently be connected to a computer looking up ways to continue living the life Robert, and I had created for ourselves. We also began discussing holistic remedies or eastern treatments. My entire life, I had never even heard of oriental medicine, but Robert was a health geek. He was regularly reading about the next big health breakthrough, and I'm glad I had him by my side to aid in my new path.

We finally arrived at home, and like children, we ran to the office to begin our research mission. My expression soon turned from happiness to anxiety within the first couple of minutes of looking at the computer screen. Both drugs Choan had recommended had a slew of side effects that appeared scarier and more detrimental than the actual disease. "How can this be?", as I thought aloud. Are medications not supposed to help the patient? It was baffling to look at the research performed on each drug. As Robert and I ran down the list of endless side effects, we both looked at each other and knew this wasn't going to work for me. Although most patients on both the drugs given to me by Choan have had positive results, I knew this wasn't going to be an option for myself or my family. Discouraged, I turned away from Robert and headed to the bedroom. Robert rolled over from his desk, and before I hit the door, he grabbed me tightly. He hugged and kissed me and said, "I'm going to do some more research on other remedies I can find that you may like"; I will never forget how even in the darkest of times Robert looks to the sky for hope. After all, I was his Wonder Woman, and he was my Superman. A sigh of relief washed over me for the second time that day, and I called Jenna to tell her about my diagnosis. I explained to her the pharmaceutical options, and then I told her I didn't want to take them. She listened to me as always and said, "Knowing Robert, he will find something that will work for you." We talked as we usually do, and she said, "you know Dawnmarie, I always knew something was wrong with you. I was kind of hoping you were crazy though because I would've loved to visit you in a padded room", We both laughed, and I said, "well, you never know when I'm going to go crazy so keep that padded room on standby." We finished our conversation, and I walked back down the hallway to check in on Robert.

As I approached, I heard Robert on the phone with his best friend, Anthony Bradley. Robert was confessing his worries about me and the final fate that originates from the disease. He continued expressing disdain for the western medication, and in his prideful voice, he told Anthony he was determined to find a treatment that would allow him and I to continue the life we had built for each other. I waited until he was off the phone, and then I walked into his office. I could see him crying from his adjacent door, and I went in and hugged him. I looked at him with a hopeful glance and said, "this isn't going to kill me. I am a fighter, and together, we will find what will work for me to fight this phantom". A week passed by, and Robert had been glued to the computer. He was compiling as much information as he could about the disease. I, on the other hand, was finally able to relax after years of worrying that I was crazy. It indeed was a sigh of relief. Our appointment day arrived, and we went back to Dr. Choan's office for our check-up. In her office, I told her I didn't want to take the medication she had suggested. She rebutted and urged me to reconsider. I said to her and Robert, "I have been on so many medications over the years; I just want my body to be clean. I want to try the natural and holistic remedy for a while and see the results from that experimentation". Choan and Robert looked at me, and they both nodded. We made an agreement on that day as well. In one year, I will return from this experiment and have another MRI performed. If my lesions had grown in that time, then I would agree to Choan's remedies, if not I would remain on the track I was. She was so respectful of my wishes. After that discussion, we began talking about the supplements and neurotransmitters that my brain was no longer producing. A significant impact on my nervous system was the lack of serotonin and norepinephrine it was producing. MS attacks two of the biggest neurotransmitters and completely drains them from your body. The imbalance would put me in a constant state of flux emotionally, mentally, and physically. To keep those levels stable, I was prescribed Cymbalta; a medication to boost my natural Serotonin and Norepinephrine levels. Serotonin is a unique neurotransmitter that contributes to feelings of well-being, happiness, and proper cognition. She also gave me Remeron to control my tremors and keep me semi-stable. Let's face it; no woman or man is entirely stable. So that was it, our meeting went well, and Robert and I walked off confident. I was happy to only be on minimal medication, which made it easier on myself and Robert.

I started taking the new drugs, and in two weeks, I began to feel happier and more relaxed. It felt like when Robert and I would be on all our incredible vacations over the years. I was finally feeling happy consistently, and it felt good. After years of endless anxiety and depression, my brain was finally getting what it needed. I really liked how the Cymbalta made me feel, and I began remembering all the incredible times Robert, myself, and the kids had made over the years. It felt like a section of my memory had been unlocked. All the happiness over the years was flowing through me each coming day. The medication wasn't a cure-all, but my phantoms soon were acting up less than they were. I would continue to have the occasional off day. I would wake up with my phantoms on occasion with some loss of vision, the burning sensation, or my inability to walk, but through all that I knew I could keep living my life the way I wanted to. Joseph was graduating from 8th grade, and I hadn't been at St. Edwards school volunteering for over a year. It was his middle school awards dinner I saw all my friends and teachers I knew from over the years.

They opened their arms to me and were so happy to see me. They all said that they had been praying for me every day to heal. They had my name on the pray list for over two years. All the kids who I had coached were so sweet and gave me a big hug. It felt so amazing. I felt like I was in the right place in my life. My mission was only starting, but it's always better to start off on the proper stride. I trusted and knew that God had plans for me. I wasn't entirely sure what they were yet, but I knew my journey was going to impact more than just my immediate family.

Chapter 51 – A New Path

After my diagnosis in 2012, I began constructing my new lifestyle. For the most part, I remained hopeful, but the days when I would have a significant attack or flair-up always brought me down. I wasn't going to let just one day stop me, so I kept pushing through my endless pain and redistributed that energy to other more critical faculties. I will always fear the worst, especially when it comes to my disease. Eventually, I know the condition will become incredibly challenging to live with, but until that time, I'm going to do my best to continue living. After all, what is a life without living it? One of the exciting prospects of beginning a holistic approach was learning how to eat and exercise properly. I had always been in the gym, but when it came to food, I was not disciplined. Robert was a big help with that, and he helped me construct an amazing paleo diet. I could eat most everything I wanted, but I had to stave from extreme sugar and inflammatory foods like fried or manufactured material. My diet consisted of lots of vegetables, and I'm talking about eating and drinking greens, fish, chicken, eggs, whole grains, fruits, water, and a slew of new foods I had never heard of. We can't forget about the occasional wine glass for the pain though. I had to stay as healthy as possible to continue living my life with multiple sclerosis. I even noticed that if I decided to cheat myself on my dieting or exercise, I would feel the ill-effects from the disease mentally and physically. We remodeled the kitchen and inserted wooden floors to signal a change for the entire family. Robert and I redesigned the house to be ready for me, so if the disease ever took over my body, and I was wholly paralyzed, everything would be more accessible to me. Robert, Robby, Simone, Joseph, and I were ready for the new path. Each of them had been prepped on ways to help me with any activity that I needed assistance in, and our family began to become even closer than I could imagine.

A couple years past and my living situation had changed entirely. All three of the kids were in high school, and they were operating their own lives without my intervention. We all remained incredibly close, except for the occasional teenage drama that would disrupt the household around 3 PM during the weekday. Robert and I even began discovering new aspects about each other that we hadn't touched on before, and it was exciting. Life was going well, and I was into my routine. The kids were self-sufficient, and this helped me focus a lot on myself. That coming summer, Simone was going into her 3rd year of high school, and her choir group was going on a trip to Germany and Austria. From all the traveling Robert and I had done before we had the kids, I had never been to Europe before. The school's choir was going touring all over eastern Europe's countryside, and I was invited as a chaperone for the trip. I was so excited to go with Simone, and I knew this trip was going to be beautiful. The tour was going to be a trip of a lifetime. I think I was even more excited about this trip than Simone. The excitement didn't halt my anxieties, unfortunately. I was very nervous about going overseas because I knew my routine that I had been grinding out for a couple years was about to be disrupted. The farthest I had traveled since my diagnosis was Hawaii, and I knew that flying put my body into a whacky state. Who knew how a fourteen-hour flight was going to affect me? I relaxed a little knowing Simone was with me, and she had always been my beautiful little caretaker. She knew how to help me when I would have attacks from having MS, and I felt confident we would be alright. If I was going to move on with my life, I needed to go and prove to myself that I could still live a happy, active life with my phantoms. This was the time to do it.

I began to imagine the hills coming alive with the sound of music, grassy hillsides, and fantastic architecture. I couldn't stop looking at pictures of Austria before we left. I especially wanted to see all the amazing churches that had been built over centuries, because I wanted to pray in every one of them. Luckily for me, I also had a free concert at each church on tour. Another exciting aspect of the journey was visiting the house and grounds from the famous movie, "The Sound of Music" by Robert Wise. This movie was one of Robert's favorite film of all time, and he loved it as a child. Robert was worried about me traveling, but I knew if I could do this, then I could do anything. It was a fourteen-day trip entirely organized by the school. The agenda was structured precisely with every hotel, concert, tour, breakfast, lunch, dinner, and bedtime. I felt secure, knowing I would have a consistent schedule. All I had to do was go and follow along.

Well, the day finally arrived, and Simone and I were ready to embark on the trip of a lifetime. Luckily, Robert had bought me business class tickets, so I had a laydown bed to rest the entire flight. This helped control my phantoms during the flight. Simone was in the economy section with her classmates, and she took some sleeping pills and passed out the entire flight. Fourteen hours flew by quick, and we landed in Germany. Once we left the airport, our tour was underway. I took over two thousand photos and videos during our trip. I couldn't get enough of the natural beauty all around me.

Every town, church, or historical site we went to had centuries of history and I bought relics from each of them. I also watched my daughter and her choir perform in front of hundreds of people. Each concert took place in some of the most famous churches around the globe. The sound was incredible, and I was so proud to be with them to hear their beautiful music. All my dreams were coming true. I was touring the world and seeing everything with my daughter. I only had one regret during the entire trip. I wish Robert and my sons were with us, in time I knew we would all visit Europe. I remember this beautiful little town called Altruppersdorf in Austria. This small town looked like it was plucked out of a fairy tale. We arrived at our hotel, and they notified us they had been preparing for our visit for over a year. They welcomed us with open arms and treated us like family.

European culture is very polite, and I loved being surrounded by such worldly people. They explained to us their town's history, and they even wore traditional clothing from centuries ago. That night, as the choir sang, I witnessed a miracle. The choir had sung their hearts out like never before. The sound echoed through the halls of the church, and it repeated in a heavenly tone. I felt a hand over my shoulder. I knew nothing was there, but I felt warm on the inside. I swear, an angel touched me that day, and I felt reassured that my new path had been the right one.

When our tour ended in Altruppersdorf, all the kids started to cry. I even shed a tear from the sheer beauty I experienced. The choir students had all made friends within the town, both children and adults alike. I will never forget the people or the place in my lifetime. We continued with the tour, and we were on our way to the famous salt mines in Austria. After the very long bus drive, we all got out and admired the beautiful lakeside at the base of the salt mine. When they said we would have to walk uphill to the mining lift, I shook my head and said to Simone, "oh shit, my booty is going to be killing me tomorrow," Simone replied, "Mom! Watch your language". We both giggled and set off with the rest of the group up a three-mile-long hill.

Yes, I took many stops to rest, but nothing was going to stop me from seeing anything on this trip. My legs burned, and they were getting weaker, but I wasn't going to let my phantoms wrangle me down. We made it to the top after an hour of walking, and we hopped into the lift. It took us up even higher, and as we glided up, I could see every hill and grassy knoll for kilometers; since I was in Europe, I can use the metric system. The air was pure, and I wish I could breathe like that all the time. Once to the top, we had to walk even more to get to the entrance of the salt mines. Wow, my booty was going to be hurting in the morning! After an hour of walking, we arrived at the opening of the mine. The tour guides told us to put on these jumpers so our clothing wouldn't contaminate the salt mine. We all made fun of each other and had so much fun doing it. As we were walking into the pits, I had zero ideas on how far we were going to go. These were all the original tunnels since the beginning of the 1800s, and I was slightly terrified and excited traveling through them. About one hour later we got to the bottom of the mountain we had just walked up. We walked down and through an entire mountain! The salt was pink in color, and we watched a movie in the middle of the magical mountain explaining its history and unique features. The tour guide then asked if the choir could sing. The choir looked around at each and formed up. They began singing, and the halls of the mine echoed with the most heavenly sound. Shortly after the singing, we were set to go sliding down the mountain on wooden logs; it was like Disneyland!

We slid down the mountain and ended up in the gift shop, how convenient. By the end of our tour, I was utterly exhausted. I worried my exertion had been too much, and I knew I needed to rest. Luckily, we met for dinner at the bottom of the mountain near the lakeside. I sat down and started to tremor; that was my first MS flare-up since I left the states. I took my medication, and we got on the bus to drive to the next town. I fell asleep, and when I woke up, we were at the next stop. It was a sigh of relief because I could get the rest I needed.

We had been to Munich, Salzburg, Altruppersdorf, and everything in-between. Now we were at our last stop before coming back to the states. We were in Vienna,

Austria. That night I slept through the fatigue because I wasn't giving up. I knew we had a lot of walking to cover over two days in Vienna, and I was ready to experience more. The first day we went into the famous church in the heart of Vienna, where the choir sang for the Sunday Mass. After that, we had an all-day tour of the city and its history. It was raining hard that day, and we didn't have umbrellas, but we didn't care. We would hide under the rooftops of the building as we toured, and the kids started to sing openly on a whim. Citizens of the city stopped in their tracks to listen to this unexpected concert; I felt like I was on a movie site. The hair on my arms was standing up, as I watched Simone sing without boundaries as they opened the heavens with their voices. That night was our "last supper"; at least that's what we called it. We had to walk up to another mountain to the castle where we would be dining. The castle had been converted into a monastery during the dark ages. When we arrived at the top, we ate like the kings and queens in medieval times. By the end of the night, three other parents and I called the nite early. I had a flair-up from all the walking and the inconsistency from the food I wasn't used to. I had to take more medication that night just to sleep. My body was starting to shut down, and I knew it was time to go home. After a very long, but incredible trip, I said some prayers to get me thought the next few days.

The next morning was free time for all of us. All the girls and I were so excited because we got to go shopping. There was only one store I really wanted to go in, and yes it was Louis Vuitton. For those of you who don't know me that well, Louis Vuitton and Yves Saint-Laurent are my two favorite fashion labels. French culture and design have always captured my eye, and I had to visit each LV store around the world to get my fix.

I waited in line for forty minutes and bought myself a sleek black handbag. It had these beautiful gold charms on it, and Vienna engraved on the bag so I would also remember this trip. This was the trip that made me stronger than ever, but I knew this was only the beginning of my journey. I began restructuring my brain again to acknowledge that even I have limits when it comes to my disease, but I was still going to do my best when it came to live the life I wanted.

We arrived back to the states after a long and unforgettable two weeks, and I was happy to be home. I was completely fatigued and exhausted. It took me two weeks before I left our house to do anything. My body wasn't allowing me to do anything. I woke up during those two weeks in immeasurable pain, but you know what? I forced myself out of bed, grabbed a cup of coffee, and kept ongoing. I had to force myself to walk even when I didn't want to because it helped me focus on other activities besides the pain. That same summer we went to our second home in Maui for another two weeks. As always, Maui was time to heal and relax from a year of stress. I felt recharged and healthy as I slept in and took naps on the beach. The sun shined on my family and me as we continued to make lasting memories.

After our relaxing vacation, I returned to my routine. I began training again, and I felt determined to continue living my life to the fullest. I made it around the world, and I felt like I had been blessed by God to carry my shield of honor. My daughter said I should start an Instagram account to promote living my life even when I struggle daily with my disease. She plugged the idea into my brain that when people look at me, I can inspire them to live their lives to the fullest. I took the message to heart, and I started telling my story to the world on Instagram. I began exposing myself to the world around me, and I documented everything. I figured that even if my message reached just one person, I could make all the difference in their lives. At first, I focused solely on recruiting other MS patients to my cause. I wanted people who were like me to see that even when we feel hindered physically, mentally, or emotionally, we can still feel beautiful, strive to be active, and spread awareness. Not many people know about MS, and over the years, I have continued to meet more amazing people just like me who are striving to make an impact just like me. My feed was simple. At first, it was mostly exercise and food to show that even the simplest of lifestyles can make all the difference. When I worked out within my boundaries, I felt good, and I wanted others to feel the same as me. I hadn't felt alone in a while, and life is meant to be shared. Robert and the family were more than supportive of my cause. My entire life I felt like I was subdued by these unknown phantoms, but now that I knew the name, I was able to become the Wonder Woman I always knew I could be. As I built my web of influence on social media, I met so many others like me. When I didn't see a post from one of my supporters or friends in a while, I would send them a note to check upon them. We established what I called my MS Family around the world.

Chapter 52 – A Bold New World

My first post was on September 17th, 2017. My daughter, Simone, was my fight photographer. She went to take photos of me working out on the pier in San Clemente, California. The first photo she took captured me holding on to the wired chains on the walkway of the pier. My caption on my first post was, "I may have Multiple Sclerosis, but it will never have me." Every journey begins with the smallest steps, and I was ready to rock'n'roll.

It didn't matter if my story was going to reach millions or a few hundred, all I cared about what making a difference in every life I touched. Luckily, I had an amazing husband who knew how to network. I learned a lot from him and began structuring an amazing feed full of local support and encouragement for not only MS patients, but also any disease that makes people feel less than themselves. I believe a condition shouldn't define a person, but a person should define the condition. My first big step, besides the simple exercise and food videos, was my exposure to the world of modeling. Ever since my first retail job and art school, I have been in love with the art of design. I thought what better way to express my everyday challenges than to start creating a powerful and beautiful feminine figure. If I was able to show that even with this disease, I can still feel beautiful and powerful than I could reach many women. Well, it worked, and my followers came rolling in. I was being contacted left and right from my closest supporters to a myriad of artists and photographers who wanted to join my mission. That December (2017) I was sent a message by a photographer named Reed. He said he could help me grow my Instagram and influence. Robert and I met with him, and I participated in my very first photoshoot ever at the age of 51 years old.

I really didn't know what to do. Reed told me to do what came naturally to me. I would ask how to move my face and body in different directions as he peered through his lens, and when we wrapped up, I looked at the photos. It never occurred to me that the female image is incredibly powerful, and when I saw myself posing, I knew my message was going to impact many women's lives. Self-confidence is incredibly hard to build in a woman and trust me; I have had years of experience building mine. I'm not perfect, nor will I ever be. I realized that my modeling instilled me with confidence, and I thought what better way to share how my lifestyle made me feel than to post myself looking like I had always dreamed. Before I knew it, I was modeling and shooting for weeks. I always wanted to model as a little girl, but I was five feet two inches. I had this image in my head that a model had to be "perfect"; she had to be tall, delicate, and exceedingly feminine. Well, I think a change in the status quo needed to happen. I was fifty plus years old, and I looked and felt good even with my phantoms raging through me every day. I could show the world that any woman or man can make themselves feel beautiful or handsome by recognizing their own self-worth and taking the chance not to let anything hold them back. Robert and I hired this photographer, and small local companies started to contact me to become an ambassador. They sent me clothing to model and post, and I learned a lot about networking. In the next few months, Robert went out and bought a camera to start learning how to be one of my photographers. He took classes and learned to capture the most perfect moments. Robert knew me like the back of his hand, and I was his muse to play with. Now he is my fulltime photographer unless I am on a professional photoshoot where they utilize their own team. Everywhere we go, Robert brings his camera everywhere, and we always have clothing stocked in our trunks. It ranged from local clothing stores to high-end fashion brands. We hit them all, and we were always prepared to capture that perfect moment. We returned to Maui the following summer and had a fantastic time. I loved having Robert taking photos of me; he was inspiring, and his smile reminded me that I was his love. I was beautiful, I was powerful, and I was fighting every day to be with him and my family. Yes, the sex kept getting better and better as well. We have both hit an incredible stage in our lives where we continue to learn from each other and admire each other's bodies and minds. Robert's heart will always be my biggest turn on because he has endless amounts for his family.

After we returned from Maui, Robert surprised me with a fantastic adventure. I remember walking to my desk in our bedroom, and I saw this petite vanilla envelope lying there. I recognized the handwriting immediately and opened the letter. Inside the envelope were two tickets to Paris, France. I rejoiced with glee, and I jumped up and down, screaming. Robert came rushing in and said, "it's just you and me baby!", then I realized the dates on the tickets. We were leaving in two days! I couldn't believe it; I had dreamed about this moment my entire life. Our trip was fast approaching, and I ran into our bathroom and begun packing. I sifted through my entire wardrobe, knowing I had to look like a Parisian, and I just decided to stuff three suitcases full of clothing. You never know when I might need a wardrobe change for a photoshoot near the Eiffel tower, right? The day came, and Robert and I embarked on an incredible journey across the pond.

Paris was incredible. As we drove into the city, I fell in love immediately. It was everything I imagined and more. I couldn't get enough; the city was like a drug, and I wanted to ingest it all. We spent a week in the most prestigious hotel but barely spent any time there. We spent our time walking everywhere. We hit all the major tourist locations, but the highlight was all the little holes in the wall. Those cafes and restaurants all had the most fantastic food. Of course, what would the trip be without photos? Well, don't worry, we took many and even created an album for it. It was the middle of June, and the weather was a little muggy, but my MS was treating me appropriately. Every evening I would nap and rest from a long day of walking the beautiful streets. When nighttime rolled around, that was a completely different story. Robert and I ran the streets red with fashion galore. I stepped out of the hotel every evening dressed in lovely gowns, and Robert was sharply dressed everywhere we went. Paris was a dream, and I was there fulfilling it. If things couldn't get any better, just wait. Robert and I made love every night, and the French romance that washed over us felt like falling in love all over again. Besides all the personal growth Robert and I experienced, my favorite part about Paris was the history and art. Since I was a child, I had always admired the masters. From Monet to Van Gogh, I saw all the works. Each art piece I looked at brought me to tears. It felt like I was in art school all over again. I sat in front of each of my favorite pieces and admired them for what felt like hours. As we walked through Le Louvre and Musee D'Orsay I analyzed each Impressionist art piece with incredible detail, and I even flexed my drawing skills. I had a petite notepad I began doodling on. Paris reinvigorated my love for art, and I started imagining what I could do with that for my newfound mission. Another highlight of the trip was the food! We ate at some of Paris' most prestigious restaurants and even ventured to little holes in the wall. Surprisingly, those holes had more exquisite food than many of the tourist traps. Every morning waking up, next to the love of my life, I would smell the nearest bakery making its fresh pastries and coffee. We sat down at a plethora of cafes and would just watch the people. I loved listening to all the French speak; their language is beautiful, but also incredibly fast spoken. My brain was a sponge, and I kept wanting more.

No matter where we would eat the food was incredible. Paris will always have my heart, and Robert and I began imagining settling down here. I never wanted to leave this magical place. I told Robert I would love to live here one day, and he agreed.

I remember one-night Robert and I were crossing the Seine, and the clock struck midnight. We both glanced to see the Eiffel tower dazzling with light, and Robert grabbed me by the waist. I was already a little bit tipsy, but I fell into his arms with grace, and he kissed me like it was the first time. If that wasn't one of the most perfect moments of my life, then I couldn't tell you what could top that. At that moment, all those years of pain, loneliness, and depression seemingly washed away as the lights of the city glowed on the two of us. Luckily, I only had two flair ups the whole time I was there. On the flight home, I turned to Robert and said I want to go back someday with the family. He looked at me and said, "anything for the love of my life," I mean come on. Could he swoop me off my feet any harder?

We arrived home, and both Robert and I missed Paris. I started returning to the mission I began before I left for vacation, and I was fully recharged. Modeling came first, and I had more local companies approach me for ambassador status. I felt so alive, and I was on track to do everything I ever imagined. I had a small relapse upon my return to my everyday routine. My eyesight was coming and going and a sharp stabbing sensation, like pins and needles, covered my body. I believe it was due to the stress from traveling and trying to get back on my time zone. I knew I needed to rest and stay home for a week before returning to such an active lifestyle. After a short recovery, I started training at RVCA with a fellow named Bryce; he was my boxing trainer. I loved boxing. It felt like it really helped me with my cognitive functions. I was moving quicker than I ever had, and I was forcing my brain to focus on driving rather than attacking me. I trained with Bryce for over six months at RVCA. Bryce was an incredible trainer and very kind. He understood my limits and how my MS worked. After training with him for a while, his wife told me that Bryce's mother had Multiple Sclerosis and had passed away. I felt honored and that he had me in his care training with me. His wife and son would come into the studio after my practice, and I would play with his son. He was so adorable and incredibly sweet, just like his Mom.

After feeling the success of boxing, my body began feeling better on a regular basis. My searing pain transformed into waking up sore in the morning; I was feeling great. Luckily, I had help with my decision to return to the gym. Ryan Dietrich, an aspiring actor, boxing coach, and excellent personal trainer. He pushes me two to three times a week at the gym mixing boxing with weightlifting and cardio; oh me, oh my, To mirror the fact that Ryan is an excellent trainer, is to explain that as soon as we met and I began to explain my diagnosis to him, Ryan performed his own research at home to understand how to train me to my fullest. He is considerate, funny, and he kicks my ass!

I came home from training one day, and Robert had another surprise waiting for me. I smiled and asked, "what surprise?", he replied, "Well, I just planned a five-week trip across Europe." I couldn't believe it; we would be leaving in one week. I was ecstatic. I went to see Dr. Choan, my trusty neurologist, and she said if I had any flair-ups across the pond, then I needed to understand my boundaries and rest frequently. I knew I could go on the trip and manage my MS because nothing was going to stop me from fulfilling my dreams I had since I was a child. Even if I had a flair-up, I could rest, take the proper medication, and move along. Multiple Sclerosis wasn't going to stop me from living my life and touring around the world.

Chapter 53 - The Tour of a Lifetime

Robert, I, Joseph, Simone, and Kyle (Simone's boyfriend) arrived at the airport on our departure date, and we were ready for an adventure of a lifetime. Robby had chosen to remain behind in California while he worked for his racing sponsor and attended a summer session at UCI to get ahead in his studies. Our first stop was Malaga, Spain. Once we arrived in Malaga, we stayed at this totally chic hotel right in the middle of the city. Our youngest son, Joseph, was going to study abroad in Spain for the summer. Malaga was so beautiful, and the Mediterranean air filled the city. Joseph would be departing from the group once we headed to our next location. We toured around Malaga for three days before we headed to Barcelona.

Once we landed in Barcelona, our driver picked us up, and Robert gave him the address. I didn't know where we were going because I wanted everything to be a surprise. We arrived at this boutique hotel, called the H10 Madison. It was located right in the middle of Barcelona. This hotel was even better than the last one, and I felt like I was in a James Bond film. It was expensive, old, and surprisingly modern. I fell in love with it. We toured all over the city; every corner was like everything I ever read about in all my history books. I couldn't get enough. I felt so alive again, I felt like a little girl dreaming of a fairy tale. It wasn't just a fairy tale for myself, because I was really living it with my husband, Robert, and our daughter, Simone, and Kyle. Robert booked a hot air balloon trip and a beautiful ride up the Mallorca mountains to a beautiful monastery. The monastery was the monastery de Montserrat; it was holy ground with the most fascinating story surrounding its long and rich history. I could feel God through every step. The peaceful aura surrounding the monastery relaxed me the entire time I was there; I could have stayed there for days. In the next two days, we continued to walk all over Barcelona.

The buildings were like something I had never seen. Whoever built these gorgeous buildings was an architectural genius. We took many photos and videos, so I would always remember the beauty. I treasure my photos so much because Multiple Sclerosis degrades a lot of the white and grey matter in my temporal lobe. This degradation hinders my ability to recall, and sometimes I lose significant amounts of time. The temporal lobe is the central storage system in our brain for memory, so I wanted everything documented. We ate an assortment of tapas and drank so many kinds of Spanish wine. How lucky was I to be able to make this trip of a lifetime? Our next stop was Nice, France, and I was even more excited to return to France. We stayed at the Hyatt Regency there. Once in Nice, it was like walking back in time. Some of the buildings were so rich with history, and we had a personal driver take us everywhere in a large van so I could lay down. After a week and a half of visiting three cities, I began having flair ups. My legs were having difficulty walking, and my entire body was so fatigued. It wasn't going to stop me. Every day I stayed hydrated, ate clean, and napped when I could. Our hotel sat right on the ocean, and our room had an ocean view of the beautiful Mediterranean. Robert had arranged to have us travel by van to Monaco for the coming day. I slept all the way to Monaco. We made one stop along the drive because the views from the cliffs were something, I would never be able to experience the for the first time, again. Robert helped me out of the van and held on to me. Simone and Kyle went down before us, and all I could hear was Simone saying, "Mom! It's so beautiful. We need to have a photoshoot along the cliff". I totally agreed with her. She took some of the cutest photos of Robert and me, even though I was struggling that day. Her smile lifted me up, and the phantoms trying to wrestle my body down were lessening their grip. It was the best day ever. We arrived back to our hotel and had a very early dinner. We called the night early, and I thought it best to rest for the upcoming adventures. Robert gave me all my medication and put me to bed. He always takes such good care of me. The next morning, we decided to stay at the hotel and rest. I laid in the sun and napped a lot. Later that night, we walked across the moonlit beach along the water. The weather was perfect, but the shore was very rocky. I mean there were rocks all over the beach. It wasn't sand, it was rocks. It was hard for me to walk on. I was losing my balance, but Robert held me like the rock he is. I said to Robert, "if anyone wants to know how it feels when our legs don't want to work right, have them walk blindfolded on this beach," he laughed and held my hand under the extravagant moonlight. Unfortunately, MS also affects our natural equilibrium, so walking on uneven makes it hard for us with this disease. However, I am so damn stubborn that I wasn't going to let it stop me. I walked with Robert's help and even jumped into the ocean. I had to model some bathing suits for a friend of ours, Hannah Reed, and this was a perfect spot to do it. Thank goodness Robert is my personal photographer because trying to walk and pose on the rocks under the water was very difficult. I kept falling over myself, but I kept a smile on my face. I could do anything I put my mind to, no matter what this disease told me I couldn't. We got some incredible shots for Hannah, and I had a good laugh shooting under the moonlit water. As I live with MS, I learned that laughing is the best recipe for making myself feel good, even when under duress. I also have an incredible natural talent to laugh at myself, so that helps.

That night we had dinner in the middle of this lively town, and everyone was out and about. We had so much fun, and laughter filled our aura of love. Every memory we made together was as memorable as the last.

Our next stop was Cannes, France. We took another beautiful ride along the coast, and our driver told us all about the history of this little village. He told us how the city became the lead site for the annual film festival, and he told us stories of each celebrity he drove. Once we arrived, we couldn't get enough of this magical town; we all loved it. Every corner, every turn, and every part of the countryside had incredible views no matter where we looked. It was truly breathtaking. Not only that even the roads we travel on were so rich in history, I felt like I was in Alfred Hitchcock's "To Catch a Thief" driving along the cliffs.

The next stop was Venice, Italy. I couldn't stop smiling; every stop on my bucket list was coming true. We took a train to Venice and arrived directly from the canal. Our tour guide picked us up and walked us to the boat taxi. We all got in, and Simone and I were so excited. Robert was talking to our tour guide while Simone, Kyle, and I were taking pictures and videos. As we got closer, I could see San Marco island, and it was a dream. The ringing bells from the churches sprinkled throughout the city echoed across the water, and it was remarkable to hear. As we came closer to the hotel, we began seeing all the little gondolas taxiing people across the water. I started to cry; I couldn't believe it. I looked at Robert and said, thank you. I couldn't conjure the words to describe how incredible our trip had been so far. I was truly blessed, and I loved experiencing every waking moment with him. He was my heart and soul, and we locked our lips as we walked into our hotel. The hotel was the Hotel Danieli, a Luxury collection from the Hyatt hotels. It was the hotel that captured one of my favorite movies, with one of my all-time favorite actresses, Angelina Jolie. The film was titled, "The Tourist" by Florian Henckel Von Donnersmarck. When we saw that movie initially, I whispered to Robert, "it would be cool if someday we could go there," well there I was in the actual hotel. I was standing there with the love of my life and our beautiful daughter. It was as stunning as the movie, even the keys were like the movie. They were real keys to, with a red tassel hanging from them. As we walked up to the stairs, I started to cry a lot. Not from my everyday phantoms, but from all, the joy I was experiencing. My heart was racing. Robert just smiled at me. He knew I was so happy with joy and awe. The room was old and covered in red velvet. Italians definitely know how to exude romance in every scene. The day we arrived was the beginning of Venice's new year celebrations. They celebrated every year on this date; it was like our 4th of July. People book years in advance to see this magical event, and we were right in the middle of it. The streets were blocked off around our hotel because fireworks were to be going off in the evening. Lucky for us, we had front row seats. We were so excited to see this spectacle and tour Venice. Over the next three days, we toured every historical site there was to see. We ate in little cafes and listened to all the people as they passed by. It was in the middle of July, and it was so hot. I bought one of the most adorable umbrellas to save me from the hot sun. Raw heat can induce an attack with anybody diagnosed with MS. Please remember to drink lots of water and keep yourself cool. For all those reading this book with MS, learning to manage your internal temperature is an excellent key to avoiding an unexpected flair-up. The food so exquisite, and we ate so much.

Surprisingly, I was losing weight from all the walking and sweating. It was a perfect and natural weight loss program. The churches we visited had lines for kilometers just to get in. Thank goodness our tour guide, he had skipped the line passes for us. I don't think I would have ever made it if we had to wait in those lines in the burning heat. At one point during the day, Robert looked at me in worry. I was going to fall from the exhaustion, and sure enough, I completely fell over. The heat and strenuous days of walking finally caught up with me. I needed to rest. We found a corner in an alley with the perfect amount of shade. The stone and brick comprising each building were so rustic and pleasant; it gave me something to look at as I rested. I drank lots of water, rest for a few, and we were back at it. We headed back to our hotel after a long day and Simone, and I aimed to take a nap. Kyle and Robert went to the gym because men will be men. After waking up, I showered, and then the four of us went out to dinner. It was our last night in the majestic city of Venice, Italy and it was everything I could have hoped for. We ate on the rooftop of our hotel, and we watched the water canals come alive with taxis and gondolas. The churches, buildings, and walkways ringed with the music of centuries passed, and it was beautiful.

Milan, Italy was our next stop, and we took a train to get there. I had never been on a train before, and it was such an awesome experience. As we blasted along the Italian countryside, I was still incredibly fatigued from our stay in Venice. However, noting how beautiful the landscape was turning out, I decided to stay up for half the ride to watch the spectacular views. Hours later we arrived at our stop in Milan. The train station was huge! We took a taxi to our hotel, The Excelsior Hotel Callia. Robert explained to me that Milan was the home to one of the most legendary artworks around the globe, The Last Supper by Leonardo Da Vinci.

I was going to experience this incredible masterpiece in person for the first time ever; I thought I was going to pee my pants. I had studied copies of the painting during my time in art school, but to see the piece in person was at the top of my bucket list. Robert just kept surprising me; it was like we were on a honeymoon all over again. After settling into our hotel, we took it easy the first day and relaxed. I thought it would be easier for me to thoroughly enjoy our trip by taking a whole day to rest in the Italian countryside. The following day, we made our way to see the epic nature of the painting. As we stood outside of the building with our tour guide, I was sweating profusely. It was hotter than Venice, and I was feeling so weak. Robert got me water, and I sat under a tree. A little later, our tour guide came to grab us; it was time to experience a dream of mine.

As we walked into the basilica that held the masterpiece, our tour guide mentioned the walls of the church stood in the middle of the city. Then he showed us photos from World War II where all the destruction caused during the fascist regime was marked. The only wall to remain upright during the siege on the city was the one with Leonardo's painting on it. As we approached another checkpoint within the basilica, the security requested we enter these special vacuum cleaners. Since the painting was an entire wall, the ambient air temperature in the room had to be preserved at a specific point to maintain the artwork. Therefore, the whole place was specially contained and sealed off from the outside. Of all the pieces I had seen during my life, I don't think I will ever admire or stand in awe from another artwork after seeing The Last Supper.

Leonardo Da Vinci was one of the most admired, studied, and reproduced artists and innovators the world had ever seen, but he had always been one of my major influences in art school. As I looked up at his incredible wall piece, I couldn't help but break down into tears seeing it. I learned so much that day. The original size of the mural was fifteen feet long by twenty-nine feet wide.

The Last Supper is easily one of the world's most iconic
paintings, and it permanently lies in a convent in Milan,
Italy. It stands as brightly today as it ever did on the wall
of Convent of Santa Maria Della Grazie. It was painted in
1495. Leonardo Da Vinci invented a new technique
during the initial process. He used specific tempera
paints on stone, then he primed the wall with material
that he hoped would accept the tempera and protect the
painting against moisture. Vibration from Allied
bombings during World War II further contributed to
part of the painting's destruction. In 1980, they began
the restoration, and it took nineteen years to complete.
All the refurbishments took place in the same room
where Leonardo da Vinci stood for countless hours, day
and months laboring over this extraordinary
masterpiece.

I couldn't stop crying. I was standing right where
Leonardo da Vinci stood hundreds of years ago. I could
feel the passion in his work as I stood in front of a pure
and unforgettable history. My body shivered and
tremored, and I wiped with tears of joy. I would have

never believed I would have been able to see my dream fulfilled, but there I was at the base weeping with joy. Robert had made all my dreams come true, and I was able to make it through the whirlwind of a journey, living with Multiple Sclerosis. Awe and joy filled my heart. I could've sat and admired the piece for days.

Someone should've just left a couple gallons of water next to me so I could try and replicate the masterpiece and imagine myself making the same strokes Leonardo had made. Kyle, Simone's boyfriend, asked Simone, "is your mom, ok? She seems so upset, and it looks like she is having tremors", Simone replied, "no, she has been waiting her entire life to see this, and those are just tearing from joy." I looked at Simone, smiled, and said, "I am standing in the same spot as Leonardo da Vinci stood." I then looked at Robert, and he held me so tight. My mind raced for hours with a myriad of emotions. By the time we got back to the hotel, I had needed a very long nap. I had been touched body, mind, and soul with raw emotion our entire trip, and it was time to rest for a long time. I fell asleep with the biggest smile on my face.

When I woke, I still had the same smile on my face, and Robert started taking pictures of me. I can remember sitting in the window of our hotel room looking out and remembering how lucky I was to see everything on this trip. As a young girl in school, I would study art history, draw, paint, and dream of the day, I would travel to see all these extraordinary and majestic pieces of art. Here I was, standing in the epicenter of the world's masterpieces. Dreams do come true, so never give up and think they will never happen. One day they will, and your life will be fulfilled.

After an awe-inspiring few days in Milan, we were packing up for our next stop. Unfortunately, Simone and Kyle were departing back to the states, because they were headed to Cabo. Oh well, this gave Robert and I more time to experience the world together. Florence, Italy was our next stop. I was so excited because we had tickets to see the statue of David, but first, we had to check into our hotel. We were staying at the Hotel Brunelleschi Firenze; it was one of the oldest buildings in Florence. It was named after the earliest owner of its time, Filippo Brunelleschi. Filippo was a wonderful renaissance author and artist of the dome of Santa Maria del Fiore. This is one of the most unique buildings in the whole Tuscan capital, and his crest marked the symbol of the hotel. We stayed in the Pagliazza Tower suite on the third and fourth floor, they performed some restorations and made it such a charming hotel; it felt like we were living back during the Renaissance.

We were in the middle of Florence, and I couldn't wait to explore this historic city. We napped from our day of traveling, then got up a few hours later to get ready for dinner. We planned to walk around to see the city at night because we had heard it rivaled the lights in Paris. Our hotel was also kind to alert us about the Gypsy community. Gypsies were densely populated throughout all of Florence, and they were masters of pickpocketing. I worried about becoming a victim to a crime, and the anxiety started an unexpected flair up. I was losing my eyesight, and a wave of exhaustion washed over my body.

My right leg became so numb, I had a hard time walking. I took some extra medication to help aid the fight, and Robert suggested we stop and rest for a little. We sat down at this wonderful café, drank some water and at some homemade Italian food to help get my mind off the stress of Gypsies. I knew I was over worrying because Robert is a very tall and powerful man, and he wasn't about to put me in any danger at all. I knew this, but my mind continued to race. To all those with any disease, anxiety, and stress all affect us differently. For me, anxiety is sometimes crippling, and can easily activate an unwanted flair-up. Part of me living with MS is managing all the little stresses and worries, but sometimes even the strongest of wills can be overwhelmed. When that happens, take the time to rest, and I believe you can get through anything once you're recovered. Stress is hard to control, and my everyday phantoms sometimes take the reins without permission, but I will never let them get the best of me. Later that day, we went to the Galleria Dell'Accademia to see the Statue of David.

The statue is unprecedented in beauty. I had read about it in school and seen pictures, but to be standing in its wake made it hard to conjure words. Michelangelo's most famous piece of art is the statue of David. This astonishing Renaissance sculpture was created between 1501 and 1504, and it stands at fourteen feet tall. Michelangelo was twenty-six years old when he created David for the Cathedral of Florence. At the time, he was the highest-paid artist. This was indeed the most groundbreaking masterpiece of sculpture. The gleaming white marble glistened in every form of light. No one expected it to be so tall and so real; every part of the body was carved and etched perfectly. They even built a museum around it! Every piece of art inside the museum was truly breathtaking and incredibly beautiful, but when the day ends, it cannot be denied that this work stands above the rest. David's influences have carried on through the palms of every sculptor, modern and Renaissance alike, to achieve the same beauty and excellence that Michelangelo completed. At the Accademia gallery, I sat and admired from a short distance the perfection of the most famous statues in Florence and perhaps the world. I reflected the days of my youth in art school, and I remembered drawing the same figures I was looking at in the flesh. Looking back on my school days, I wish I could go back in time to see all my old art teachers and tell them I saw everything I ever dreamed about. I can imagine showing them pictures and discussing how magical it was from the slight differences in my studies to the original artwork. I believe they would have cried tears of joy, knowing I finally made it. I was able to experience these spectacles with my husband after so many years after graduating from school. Art has always made me feel confident, smart, and unique. What better place to create and explore one's imagination than here? I would like to take this time as well to express my eternal gratitude for Robert. He made our trip of a lifetime an unforgettable experience, and all my dreams come true since our first meeting. Luckily, my body was strong enough to witness every second, every minute and hour of our trip. I will forever have these memories in my mind, heart, and soul.

After walking around the Galleria all day, my legs were becoming fatigued. Again, my body was trying to fight back. The next day we slept in and relaxed. We walked around the streets at our leisure and experienced the beautiful city. I loved walking and eavesdropping into people's stories passing by. I couldn't understand them, but it was lovely to listen to. I think I smiled every day of our trip, even though the pain I was feeling. My MS was really starting to flare up even more so towards the end of our journey, but I was so determined to see everything. I remember we stopped in this little shop. Everything inside was handmade leather goods from coats, to handbags, shoes, and boots. I even bought two pairs of shoes. They felt like no other leather that had ever been on my foot. They are the most comfortable pair of boots I'll ever own. Robert purchased a man bag, and it was super cool.

We then went to a café and sat down for lunch. A lovely gentleman, who was born and raised in Florence, Italy, overheard Robert and I talking about all our adventures and he leaned over to ask us where we were from. Robert said California, and he turned closer to us and asked where specifically? Robert replied with the name of the small town we lived in, Dana Point. The gentleman then introduced himself to us and said, "I was just there! My dear friend opened a pizzeria in the same city". We couldn't believe it. Even halfway around the globe, an Italian had ventured to the little town we called home. He proceeded to give us some names of local places around Florence to go for dinner. He told us that tourists would never even hear of these places, and we thought it would be exciting to escape the tourist arena.

When we got back to our hotel, we asked the concierge if they knew about these restaurants? They said yes, so they made a reservation for us that very night at nine. I loved eating late at night, the atmosphere was always perfect no matter where we were in Europe. I really enjoyed the evening because that meant wine time. The wine would relax me and help reduce the everyday pain I was experiencing from my phantoms. Nothing was going to stop me from living my life, and I will take whatever I can to help to mellow out the everyday pain I feel. The phantoms might break me down, make me cry, or paralyze me, but I am a fighter, and I would do everything I could to win the battle between my brain and body. On the way to dinner that night, we walked through a famous street named after one of the most powerful families in Italy, the Depeche's. It was incredible to see the hidden passageways and hear all about the secret stories. Our tour guide was unique, and her bright red hair shined throughout the day. She was very petite and incredibly knowledgeable. I loved her and the way she spoke to us with such passion. She would hold her head up high even though she was four-foot by ten. She walked like she was six-feet tall. You could tell that she loved her job and she was proud of her history. All our tour guides were unbelievable with their knowledge of Florence, Italy. I fell in love with this city and all it offered.

We had only two more days in Florence, so we hired another tour guide to take us to Cinque Terra. It was going to be a very long ride to get there, so we had a van take us. I was able to sleep and rest up for another great day. Robert had his camera ready because he knew I wasn't going to miss this excellent opportunity to take photos there; well, we ran out of storage that day from how many photos we took. I guess the mission was a success. We drove down tight and windy streets while the hillsides decorated our surroundings. The buildings were rustic and small. The alleyways were old and forged from bricks. Extravagant flowers and plants painted the walls with color, and wine vineyards sprinkled the countryside.

Most of the people who were born there still lived there. Each family would pass the home down to their children. We stopped by this little church along the way, it wasn't open, but it was stunning to look at. It sat on top of the mountain overlooking the beautiful ocean. We saw this adorable young couple who must have just been married seated on a bench overlooking the sea and admiring the view. I thought it would be such a fantastic spot to take some photos, so Robert took some on that mountain. I imagined it was like our first time after our wedding, and it was another honeymoon all over again. As we were walking back down to the village, we saw the ocean and the beach full of people. This beach was also full of rocks, but it was clearly beautiful and breathtaking. We walked through this long old tunnel to get to the next village and stopped by all the little shops to buy small souvenirs to bring home. I would love to go back there again someday. Every minute spent there was perfect, and I will never forget it. The sun was going down, and I was completely fatigued, and everything was on fire. Thank goodness I took a pillow with us, and I slept on Roberts's lap on the way back to Florence. We had one more day in Florence before we left for our next destination. That following morning, I slept in because my body was in so much pain. I was taking an extra medication just trying to get through the day. I packed our bags, and we had breakfast. We walked around the town one more time just to absorb every little detail. Florence was stunning. That following afternoon we were catching a flight to Rome.

Ok, so I love traveling in Europe. The transportation there is outstanding. The wide variety of transport made it incredibly easy for us to travel between countries and towns; I wish the US had similar transit.

We arrived in Rome, and our driver was waiting for us to take us to our last destination. Every hotel we stayed at was incredible, but this hotel in Rome was so beautiful. It was called the Eden Hotel, and it was right in the middle of the city next to the famous Spanish steps. We went to our room, and the view of the town was beautiful. We unpacked and got ready for the fastest tour ever. We only had twenty-four hours in Rome, so we were prepared to make a run for it. We asked the concierge for the quickest route to seeing everything famous in Rome. We started at the Spanish steps and went from there. At the top of the steps, you could see everything from the colors to people enchanting the city.

I felt whimsical at the top of the steps, and I had on the boots Robert brought for me in Florence. They fit like a glove, were super cute, and I had on a beautiful dress full of color with big beautiful flowers on it to match. Simple pearl earrings hung from my lobes, and my hair was super curly. I caught Robert just staring at me in awe as I swayed with the wind and twirled with delight. Shortly after he said, "Wow, I am the luckiest man in the world," and I replied, "you're damn right." Robert was rocking his cool man bag we bought in Florence, and he fit in perfectly with the Italian crowd. We went down the stairs to the next famous spot. On the right of us was the Column of the Immaculate Conception of Mary; it was so tall and beautiful. I took many photos for myself and for my mother. The next stop on the rush tour was St. Peter's Basilica at the Vatican. It was unbelievable, and magic filled the air. I felt honored to even step on such holy ground. I truly felt like I was being blessed by God. The feeling I got standing on such holy grounds felt like a light beaming from heaven above. We walked all around to see everything. I didn't want to leave, but we had so many stops to make before the end of the day. I was getting so tired from all the running and walking, but I wasn't going to let it stop me. We ordered an Uber to take us to the next stop. It was Castello Sant'Angelo city brigade and next to it the famous Colosseum. It was larger than I ever imagined. Even though it was falling apart, standing in front of it was flawless. I closed my eyes and imagined going back in time when they held the gladiator battles inside of the Colosseum. If you have seen "Gladiator" by Ridley Scott with Russell Crowe, then you can also imagine precisely how I felt being there. After the Colosseum, we walked and found a trail to explore. The trail was located directly next to the magnificent site. As we were walking up the mountain, we had two very tall men following us. Robert and I stayed close to each other and kept walking. They tried to talk to us, and all I could think of was them setting us up to pickpocket. Ok, so this is where I got proactive and turned into Angelina Jolie, a.k.a. My superhero. The man kept trying to get us to talk to him, and I could feel there were 2 other men next to me trying to get close. They kept asking questions, and we didn't answer them. I looked at the very tall guy, and stared in his face and said, "NO! Go away!". We walked faster up the hill, then we saw a man selling water bottles, and Robert asked for two. I gave him five euros for the water. It was two for three Euros, he thought he was keeping the change. I said to him, "hey, you need to give me my two Euro back. That is my change", He said no then I got in his face, and he finally gave me my two Euro. I said in probably the snarkiest voice I had every fabricated, "I know what the money means, and you can't steal for me." Robert almost started laughing, but he knew I wasn't going to let this one go. I was so proud of myself for fighting for my pocket change, and I couldn't stop laughing. I kept joking about that I was going to be the next Lara Croft, Tomb Raider. I looked to Robert, and I was like, "don't mess with me" he looked back and replied, "Oh, trust me. I know," We both cracked up.

On a side note, I am a huge fan of Angelina Jolie, and sometimes I believe I can do everything she does in her movies. Ok, I am dreaming, but who said I couldn't imagine it anyways?

Well back to Rome, and on the hill, Robert and I put together mini photoshoot. The photos came out exceptional! The dress was from a local company I modeled for back home titled, Piajie. We had two more stops to make on our rush tour; the first was the famous bridge Castel Sant'Angelo Engelsberg. The Angels decorating the bridge were as angelic as you can imagine. The next stop was for our son, Robby. He works for Dainese/AGV, an Italian motorcycle fashion company, and the companies largest store was there in Rome. We went in, took a photo for him, and brought him some one-of-a-kind t-shirts from the Rome store. After an incredible day of sightseeing, we went back to the hotel Eden and took a nap. I was so fatigued, but it was our very last night in Rome, and my Phantoms were not going to STOP Me. I looked in the mirror and said, "not today Multiple Sclerosis!" I put on some very sexy lingerie and walked out to the bedroom. Robert's eyes widened in awe, and his jaw dropped. You can imagine what occurred next. During our lovemaking, I whispered in his ear, "thank you for loving me so much and always standing by me in the good times and the bad times." He held my face and said, "baby, can't you tell we were made for each other and no matter, you'll always be by my side for Eternity."

We got ready for dinner, and I had on an elegant black dress; it was so beautiful. We went to Eden's lounge and had some early drinks before dinner. It also and impeccable spot for another photo shoot. Robert took some impressive photos of me in the bar. I was channeling my inner Angelina Jolie, and I posed for the camera felt like I was in a James Bond film. After some tantalizing talk and drink, it was time for dinner. We had the best table in the restaurant that evening. The city of Rome rotated around us, and the open windows whistled with a lovely summer breeze. It was so romantic. The sun was setting on a perfect day as we laughed and enjoyed our final night in Europe.

Chapter 54 – The Road So Far…

Our trip back home was excellent. I slept the entire way. Once we arrived on familiar shores, my body began signaling to me that it was time for a much-needed rest. I had been running on pure adrenaline from all excitement and wonder, and now I was feeling the comedown. Thankfully, ever second spent over in Europe with the love of my life will never be forgotten, and I cannot wait for the next continuing adventure. After coming home from Europe, I had a significant flare-up that almost destroyed me. I let my emotions get the better of me, and I had one of the worst Multiple Sclerosis attacks I had ever had. It paralyzed me for a week. Robert had to carry me from the bed to the bathroom because I was immobile. He fed me, laid me down, and picked me up at my beckoning call. I was completely motionless, and my speech was so broken and slurred; I wasn't masking any sense. I prayed for peace in my heart to grant me the strength to fight my way back. It took me months to find my way back to where I was before leaving for Europe. I had to stay positive, I had to keep calm, and most of all, I placed myself as the utmost importance. Sometimes selfishness can be overlooked when it comes to healing. I began therapy three times a week, and I also had massage therapy on the docket. Massages helped my muscle memory link my brain synapses to unblock all the channels that had been on fire and unused for a while. Paralysis felt like I was living a horror movie. I was unable to control anything, I had zero movements across my entire body. Thankfully after such a strenuous attack, I was able to fight back again because I am here to stay and make the difference I have always strived for. I live in varying amounts of pain every day, along with everyone else afflicted by this disease called Multiple Sclerosis. I will continue to fight and have my voice heard for all of us fighting for theirs every day. I will fight for you to my last breath. Thank you for following me along this journey so far, and with your help, I hope to continue fighting my phantoMS and making a difference in the world because we are all warriors in our own right. My name is Dawnmarie Deshaies; I am a Multiple Sclerosis Warrior, I am MStrong.

Bonus Material

Listed below is a compilation of ideas and thoughts when it comes to living with Multiple Sclerosis. These thoughts weren't going to fit in the book's main storyline, so here is a peek at my daily life and the symptoms I deal with.

My Daily Routine – Thoughts to boost positive thinking and aid in living a healthier and happier life after being diagnosed with Multiple Sclerosis:

- ✓ Being Positive was something I had to learn, don't be afraid to share your fears and anxieties with the ones around you
- ✓ Affirm to yourself that your life is worth every second spent on this world because, without you, the people around you have no hope to look for!
- ✓ Exercise your mind and spirit, meditate!
- ✓ Learn how to prepare your days, but keep your spontaneity to keep the spice of life
- ✓ Make significant life changes for the better, sometimes you need to let go to move on.

- ✓ Learn to recognize your own fears and accomplishments, try to one-up yourself each time.
- ✓ Don't make excuses, just keep moving any way you can.
- ✓ Refrain from hiding the truth, truth is the light of life. Truth brings people closer to your understanding and perspective.
- ✓ Stress is a part of everyday life, focus on the eustress because those build positive affirmations. When overcome in an unhealthy, stressful situation never be afraid to walk away or focus on the positive.
- ✓ Train your brain to handle MS flare-ups
- ✓ Spend time to recover mentally and if you're able to find the therapy that works for you albeit talking with a psychiatrist, psychologist, licensed social worker, or family and friends (only for listening, rarely for advice).
- ✓ You will fail, but they will all be learning experiences. Make the best of them. Remember the glass is always half-full.

- ✓ Develop your own healthy way of living. You do what makes you achieve more; comfort might not always be an option. Everybody is different!
- ✓ Develop a food plan
- ✓ Learn to let go of the past and not hold onto to phantom pains
- ✓ Never be afraid to ask for help
- ✓ You are the embodiment of hope for those around you, never lose sight of that
- ✓ Always love yourself first and foremost to become a light for others to live positively.

Personal Qualities I Attribute to Myself:
My Strengths:
- ✓ Compassionate
- ✓ Artistic
- ✓ intuitive
- ✓ Gentle
- ✓ Wise
- ✓ Loving
- ✓ Compassionate

✓ Naturally groovy

✓ Romantic with art, fashion, and music

✓ Spirituality

✓ Hope

My Weaknesses:

✓ Fearful of the unknown

✓ Overly trusting

✓ Sad Sometimes

✓ I have a desire to escape Reality

My Dislikes:

✓ Know it all's

✓ Being criticized, living in the past,

✓ Cruel people, especially to people who inflict pain on others and animals

This is only a minimal list of the afflictions that MS causes:

✓ Acetaldehyde Damage Brain Function

✓ Impaired Memory Loss (Destruction of Temporal Lobe over time)

✓ Decreased Ability to Concentrate (a.k.a. Brain fog)

✓ Extreme Depression and Increased Anxiety

✓ Personality Shifts

✓ Lethargy, Apathy, Heightened Irritability, Decreased Mental Energy

✓ Decreased Sensory Acuity

✓ Impaired Hearing & Speech

✓ Decreased Sex Drive

✓ Increased PMS and Breast and Body Swelling in Women

✓ Elevated rates of Infertility (Men & Women)

During one of my attacks, I feel most of the listed bullet points above. To add even more damage, our nervous system is slowly degrading from our own white blood cells eating away at our Myelin Sheath (The insulation conduit around each bundle of neurons throughout the body). Once the Myelin is peeled away, the neuron fires uncontrollably until it burns out from overexposure to electrical energy. This causes our bodies to feel like they are on fire during an attack. Us living with the disease rarely having any warnings when an onset of attacks is peering through the veil, but as we continue to live and fight, we become more attuned to our bodies. We can prepare for an attack with the available tools, but when most of the damage is internal the most, we can do is rest it out. It is an emotional and mental roller-coaster. Slowly, I strive to find my way back after an attack. Little by little, I gain back strength in my legs and arms. I also practice recalling memory, so my brain can form new pathways of recollection. I practice my speech as well, so I can carry conversations. Recovery is a slow process, but we are all warriors, and we can fight this disease. For example, I had no energy to go to the gym before leaving for our trip to Europe. I had been training five days a week before leaving, and I was in the best shape of my entire life. Natural exercise helped me concentrate on the good. I was happy and felt strong enough to go abroad.

As you can see from two chapters back, even when we are in or near heightened physical stamina, I was still susceptible to an attack. In my case, the gym is the best thing to do when I am trying to get back on track. It helps manage my depression, and my body naturally releases endorphins, which help with the various hormones and anxieties.

I am thankful for my struggles because, without them, I wouldn't have stumbled across my strengths. You are your own superhero. Never let anyone destroy your passion, courage, and vision when striving to make your life better. Our destiny is what we make it. Today, I am here writing this book. Today, I am designing a clothing line for everyone fighting Autoimmune Diseases to show that even underneath our skin, we are beautiful. Robert and I have opened a non-profit organization called Sea Warriors, and we hope to continue to fight together through the pooling of our resources and connections to help aid us in research and awareness. We aim to build a community of love, strength, and hope. Along with 2.9 other million people around the world, I am a Multiple Sclerosis Warrior, I am Dawnmarie Deshaies.

I originally created this piece of artwork to act as the original cover for the book. During our production, my editor and I decided it be best if we use an actual photo of myself instead, so we relegated it her for your viewing pleasure. This painting will be included in my first clothing collection, which will be launching soon. If you are interested in my other works and look to inquire about future art pieces or commissions, please contact me at my business email located on the back cover!